A MEMOIR OF LOVE, LOSS, AND
THE DANCE WITH DEMENTIA

GET
in the
BOAT

DARLENE FUCHS

Based on the Journals of Richard Sonnichsen

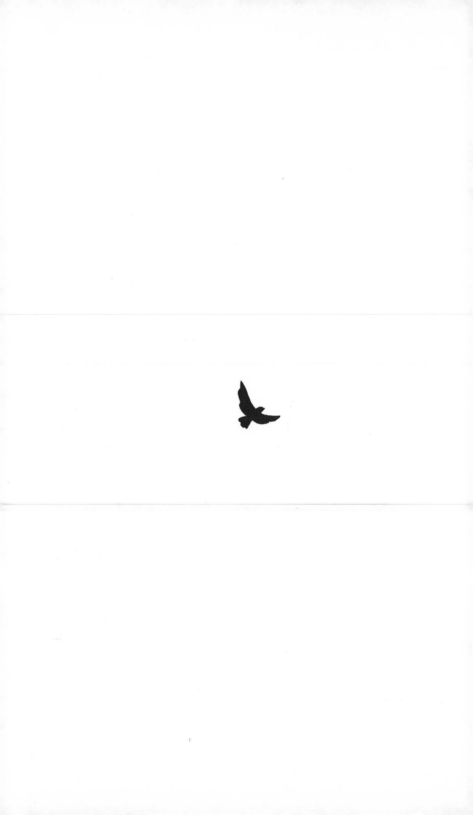

Praise for

Get in the Boat

"As a neurologist, I observe many patients and their families enduring the devastating effects of dementia. Darlene has captured the essence of the experience of the family members who have chosen to navigate the course of the complex illness with love and respect. *Get in the Boat* is a fascinating story of human resilience in the face of uncharted waters. I highly recommend it."

-Daniele M. Anderson M.D.,
American Board of Psychiatry and Neurology

"*Get in the Boat* is a true gem for caregivers, offering an abundance of wisdom, no matter where you are on your caregiving journey. Having spent 10 years in the senior caregiving community, I was absolutely captivated by the fresh insights and reassuring advice this book provides in navigating the complexities of dementia care."

-Vicki Striegel, MBA, LNHA
Licensed Nursing Home Administrator

"*Get in the Boat*, a caregiver's journal turned memoir, tells us exactly how a caregiver lives and feels yet still gives us something positive to hold on to. Giving us a behind-the-scenes look at the daily roller coaster of emotions a caregiver lives through is not only honest, it's refreshing. In a world where honesty often seems to be synonymous with sadness, this memoir stands out by presenting the raw realities of caregiving without overwhelming the reader with despair."

-Jennifer Fink "The Caregivers Caregiver"
and Host of the Fading Memories podcast

Dedication:

Dad, this journey would have been impossible without you by my side. In moments when the challenges felt overwhelming, it was your voice in my mind that pushed me forward.

I have fulfilled my promise to you; I've penned the pages of your book. May you now find peaceful repose in the embrace of heaven's splendor.

Table of Contents

Foreword: **1**
Helen Brown

Prologue   **3**

Chapter One   **6**
A New Normal

Chapter Two   **16**
Love and Golf

Chapter Three   **29**
My Job

Chapter Four   **37**
Family

Chapter Five   **52**
Intimacy

Chapter Six   **60**
Bright Light in the Sky

Chapter Seven   **69**
Hand in Hand, We Walk

Chapter Eight   **78**
It Takes a Community

Chapter Nine   **87**
Many Hands

Chapter Ten   94
Longest Day in Years

Chapter Eleven   102
Words for the Soul

Chapter Twelve   111
Stay in the Boat

Chapter Thirteen   117
Less is More

Chapter Fourteen   122
A Shared Language

Chapter Fifteen   128
Mightier than the Sword

Chapter Sixteen   134
Wings over the Water

Chapter Seventeen   141
Together, Always

Chapter Eighteen   147
The Eternal Flicker

Chapter Nineteen   153
In Sickness and in Health

Chapter Twenty   159
Waves upon Another Shore

Epilogue   165
Boat in the Harbor

Photos of Richard and Gail   175

Acknowledgements   183

Foreword
Helen Brown

I am delighted to share my foreword/testimonial for the book 'Get in The Boat'.

I met Richard through my work at Pathway Senior Living; he was my pen pal. At the time, I was a Positive Approach Care trainer and had recently returned from Australia, where I was studying Dementia Care. My job at the time was to train team members on how to approach and engage with people living with dementia. Richard and his wife (Gail) lived at The Victory Centre of Bartlett, which did not have a dementia care unit. Richard chose to stay in an apartment and care for his wife.

For several months, Richard wrote to me about his day-to-day challenges as a caregiver, and I encouraged him to continue writing to me and journaling. As I had promised Richard, I went to The Victory Centre of Bartlett to meet him and Gail in person. We talked about what it was like to live with someone with dementia and how, if we just met the person where they were and understood that they may not know our name, but they do remember how we make them feel, it would change the relationship for the better.

I spent some time with Gail, listening to music and focusing on her abilities. A few weeks later, Richard called my cell phone to let me know that Gail had started speaking again—only a few words, but she was speaking again. From the moment I got the call, I knew that Richard understood what it meant to meet Gail where she was. Richard's excitement and understanding grew, and he started writing a skit called "Get in the Boat." Richard and I would perform the skit for the entire team that worked for Pathway Senior Living. After the skit, Pathway Senior Living and Richard presented me with an award: 'Care to Know and Make it Matter'. I didn't deserve the award; Richard did.

The book beautifully captures the essence of meeting people with dementia where they are in the present moment. It emphasizes the importance of genuine connection, understanding, and love throughout the journey. It reminds us that despite the difficulties, those living with dementia can still lead fulfilling lives as long as we are willing to get in the boat.

I highly recommend this heartfelt and enlightening book to anyone seeking inspirational dementia care. Its wisdom and practical advice will undoubtedly leave a lasting impact on readers, urging us all to embrace the journey and love our loved ones through every step of it. JUST GET IN THE BOAT!

Helen Brown

President – The Pointes Consulting LLC, Positive Approach Care Trainer, Dementia MDS Coordinator, Healthcare Management

Prologue

On March 24, 1956, in the small town of Clinton, Connecticut, I watched a woman walk slowly toward me in a long, white dress of lace and satin. Her name was Gail Wagner then. As she walked, a snowstorm raged around Clinton Baptist Church, where we huddled with family and friends, but I only saw her.

Our story had begun during high school—a romance that blossomed over shared moments and shared dreams—moments and dreams that had weathered some small tests by then and led us to make promises to each other. When she reached me at the end of that aisle, a pastor spoke to us words about the union we were entering: a holy union, an eternal union. Then Gail and I repeated those words. I gave her a ring, and she gave me her life.

With us in that sanctuary was a cake topped with the figures of a bride and a groom embraced by wedding bells and two doves.

Two doves protected from a raging storm.

Gail said I do, and so did I. But before that, we said something else, buried within the vows we each accepted—words that I would not fully appreciate until much later in our story.

"…in sickness and in health, until death do us part."

Two doves, naive and innocent, we winged out into the world. There were many storms, but we were never left unprotected.

CLINTON, March 28—Mr. and Mrs. Richard Sonnichsen at their reception following the wedding, Saturday, March 24, in the Clinton Baptist church. Mrs. Sonnichsen is the former Miss Gail Wagner of Beach Park road, Clinton.

Chapter One
A New Normal

It is now 3:45p.m. Gail whispering about how bad I am.
She just whispered, "I have to get out of here".

I stood quietly at her bedside. The dim morning shadows played at her eyelashes and touched the gentle lines of her face. Her soft, whispered breaths counted out the rise and fall of her chest. I'd been standing there for some time and realized I was breathing in sync with her. This was my Gail—wife and mother to my children, my beautiful best friend, my queen. She was so peaceful and still, so like herself. I could almost pretend she was just as she ever was, that we were not really at Victory Centre but back in our family home, experiencing life just as we always had.

She opened her eyes, and the dream was gone.

"Who are you?" she asked, her voice groggy but clear. Sometimes it was most steady when her memory was least so. But I would take a few unscrambled words from her whenever they came.

"I'm your husband, Richard." I smiled wide, hoping my cheerfulness might crack the shell.

"Oh…" came her answer, but her eyes glared suspiciously.

"Let's get you up, Gail." I took a breath and moved to place a gentle hand on her shoulder. She recoiled from my touch.

"I'm Gail!" she rebuked me.

"That's right. You're Gail, and I'm Richard, your husband. Remember?"

"Oh." Eyes still glaring.

"Come on, Gail. It's time for breakfast. Are you hungry?"

I reached below the blanket for her hand but was too slow. She yanked free, and a sneaker met the side of my head, stunning me for a moment. I stepped back and shook the fog clear, then took a deep breath, trying to regain composure. How difficult it must be to fall asleep confused, only to awaken and discover a stranger in your bedroom. The thought hurt me, for her as much as myself, a reminder of our present hardships.

I threw up my hands in mock surrender and gave a lighthearted smile. At least it wasn't a knife; I lifted a quick prayer of gratitude. So far, those disturbing behaviors were left behind us at Hunt Club. Still, I reminded myself not to start Gail's day within swinging range.

"Alright," I said in my calmest tone. "That's ok. We can take our time. Why don't you give me the shoe?"

"What?" Gail's scowl gave way to confusion. She stared at the object in her hand like someone else had put it there, then set it on the bed, shaking her head and muttering sounds that weren't words, at least not ones I understood. When her eyes found mine again, they were full of Gail's essence once more.

"Husband," she said, with a touch of emotion in her voice, like she had just returned from a long trip.

My eyes dampened. "That's right," I said.

She reached for my hand and pulled me into a hug. She was so strong. She always had been, and in so many ways, stronger than me. She hadn't lost that.

We remained locked in each other's embrace until I felt one of our stomachs rumbling, reminding me of the breakfast I'd heated growing cold in the microwave. Before we could get to that, Gail needed cleaning. She let me help her out of bed, and to my relief, the mess was not as bad as it often was. But there was a downside to that benefit. Her digestion had slowed over the last week; constipation was uncomfortable in ways she could no longer describe with words. Instead, worsening behavior showed me how she felt. I would have welcomed more to clean up in the morning if it meant more relief for my Gail. Yet even so, I thanked God for that little reprieve for me.

In the shower, Gail was helpful, playful even—a welcome surprise, and it warmed me. I hadn't stopped being a man after all, even if my wife didn't remember me half the time. I longed for affection. The smallest gesture; a pat on the shoulder, the touch of her hands cupping my face, even a fleeting smile, were like a trickling spring during the droughts of nurturing.

After she was cleaned and dressed, I led her to our small dining table beneath the window, and she gifted me a smile. I left for our kitchenette to reheat her breakfast. In that moment, my thoughts drifted to the dedicated staff who worked tirelessly downstairs as the microwave plate spun and hummed in the background. The dining hall kitchen was a short trip down one flight of stairs, one of the many unexpected blessings of moving from Hunt Club Apartments to Victory Centre. I wasted no time making friends with the kitchen staff. Theirs was a thankless job, particularly in a place like this, as I witnessed day in and day out. Whenever I remembered, I told them how important they were to us, emphasizing the profound positive impact they had on my wife's quality of life. If my friendliness encouraged them to be extra generous with portions and attentive to special orders for Gail, that was just fine.

"Who are these people?" Gail murmured, pulling me back to the present.

I paused in front of our microwave. "I'm your husband, Richard," I said, more exploratory than an answer. I braced for what would come next.

She froze, no response, not even a simple turn of the head. "Gone again," she muttered beneath her breath to no one, no one visible at least.

Since arriving at our new apartment, there had been less of the paranoid behavior and violence—the sneaker incident this morning, an outlier, was a far cry from the worst behaviors at Hunt Club. Hunt Club was near the beginning of it all, our first attempt at life after the signs began. It was a good place. Our apartment was big enough, and we could afford it. There was a small library, a recreation center with activities and other like-minded people we connected with. I thought it would be a place Gail and I could comfortably retire in. I was so naive. Within months of moving into Hunt Club, I got my first glimpse of just how challenging our future would become when I returned home and found my wife brandishing a blade.

"Gail, are you okay?" Fear gripped me as I considered the possibility of someone attempting to break in while I was away.

I rushed to take the knife and hold her, but instead of melting into the safety of her husband's arms, Gail thrust the knife towards me. I stopped in my tracks, directing my gaze towards the weapon's point. An intense pang of both alarm and anguish pierced my heart. Had she not backed away in fear as she defended herself, that might have been our final day together. Hunt Club was not at fault for our situation; they were merely an apartment complex tailored for independent seniors. What we needed was help.

The microwave ding brought me back to the present at Victory Centre and the gloriously less exciting life we now lived. As I stirred her scrambled eggs and cream of wheat, my attention remained divided with one eye always on her. During breakfast, I no longer felt like Richard, the husband. I'd become Richard, the intruder, an unwelcome presence in a world inhabited solely by Gail and her invisible co-conspirator. I wondered why her disease took her there. Was it safe from the real world she no longer understood? Oh, I wished to have her back. But that wasn't the real world either. Here we were in the growing familiarity of odd happenings, and the reality we had always relied on before was fading away.

I understood little of what she said when she was "away." Most seemed to be about whoever she thought I was. Occasionally, a few clear words would slip through. Sometimes I was accused by the identity as "him" or "the man." But if ever she called this villain "Richard" to her invisible accomplice, and I answered with a "That's me!", a sideways glower was her stock punishment. Sometimes I knew who she spoke to because a stray name or clue would surface from her mumbles—a family member, her sister, or mother. Others, I didn't recognize. Charlie was a common invisible guest, and I never learned who that was. This morning, there was no identity, and that was usual.

After a spell, her disgruntled conversation fell away, and hunger gradually stole her focus. As she turned her attention to her plate, I seized the moment to engage her, attempting to bridge the divide between us.

"How are you feeling, Gail?"

She didn't acknowledge me, not even a fleeting glance. I nodded. I was still the villain. But she was still my bride, and I would always care for her no matter what.

That delicate balance was always on my mind. I watched her eat, landing one spoonful out of three, the others finding shirt or lap, falling back onto plate or table. *Should I step in?* was a question I asked myself at every meal. Nutrition was vital, and every bite lost was full of valuable calories and nutrients. Was it worth peeling away another layer of her already fragile independence?

I let her find her own way through breakfast and was proud of how much she managed to get down. That was a good sign, the experts told me. In situations like these, constipation tended to worsen with age, and appetite served as a reliable indicator for those who were unable to express themselves with words. I clung to the hope that her digestive system would soon find relief. And hopefully, there would be a positive shift in her mood as well.

I took her empty plate, and she resumed conversation with our unseen guest, pausing only when I came back for her napkin and to wipe up. I took her hand, which she received like a prisoner accepting cuffs, and guided her to the recliner, her favorite seat. I sat nearby. Her chatter started again; more mumblings broken by occasional clarity. Complete sentences had become increasingly rare, an absence that pained me deeply. We had always talked through our problems and enjoyed the many profound and mundane topics married couples often engage in. We leaned on each other in hard times and shared each other's joys during the good ones. There were plenty of both, and we were stronger for all of it; we were stronger when we were together. How much I would have given just to ask what she needed and have her tell me in simple words. Communication, once taken for granted, became an unattainable treasure.

Over the next hour or so, I might not have been present at all for the little Gail noticed me. At times, she was serious—long stretches of scrunched eyes and noises that sounded aimed more than communicated. Then something would switch. Laughter would brighten her face, and she would sit taller in her chair, smiling, sharing some pleasant memory I dearly hoped was of me or us together. This continued until her therapist arrived in the early afternoon. I usually stayed to observe as she worked with Gail. Any clue from these sessions, a new way to communicate, might unlock some small improvement in our quality of life. But our fridge was nearly empty, so while another cared for her, I left for provisions.

Forty-five minutes later, I returned. My hands were full as I paused outside the door, listening. There was nothing. No sounds. No clues to what I might find inside. The bags crinkled around my wrist as I turned the knob and peered through the opening to find a changed Gail.

"There's my husband!" a familiar voice greeted me as I used my butt to push open the door.

I don't think I could have stopped myself from smiling if I tried. I set the bags down in the entrance and walked to my wife as she took up the last remaining step between us. As we embraced, she whispered "I missed you" in my ear, in the way she had done so many times throughout our life. There might not have been more in those words than a simple lucid moment, just the normal response to a husband returning from a quick trip to the store. But I felt the weight of years. I closed my eyes and told her I missed her too and held her tight, like I would never let her go. Eventually, I leaned back and took in the sight of my wife, enjoying every detail that made her uniquely beautiful. She smiled and said, "I'm hungry."

The upturned mood was still there when I returned from the dining hall and placed lunch on the table. I asked if she liked each thing on the plate, and she smiled and nodded her approval.

"How do you like the sweet potatoes?

"Very good," she said—the same answer given for the sliced pork and the apple crisp. Lunch crescendoed to the tune of a clear-as-day "thank you" as I picked up her empty plate. I swiftly attended to the dishes, my aging fingers moving with a sense of urgency so as not to miss a moment of this bliss, and rushed back to her side. She looked up at me, and a different face had replaced my Gail's. It happened so fast.

This face was not new. I had been a constant, dark shadow at Hunt Club. Twisted and contorted—someone seeing this for the first time might believe they were seeing demonic possession.

There were so many versions of Gail throughout her dementia journey. A version would break through, stirring memories of my precious wife, transporting me to better years. Others…I couldn't imagine where they came from—primal, awful fits of rage that would engulf her, removing any resemblance to the love of my life, replacing her with something I couldn't know.

I pushed through the pain, a metaphorical knife twisting in my stomach, and forced a smile as I asked this distorted version of Gail if there was anything she needed.

"Bad…" she croaked. "Always bad to me…"

The rest of the afternoon was beset with highs and lows, each one higher or lower than before. Laughter was no longer soft and glowing but teetered on the edge of hysteria. Hostile shouting replaced the previous irritated grumbling. These turbulent waves of behavior battered us throughout the day. Upon returning from a trip to the bathroom, I found her chair vacant. I turned just in time to avoid the incoming assault of my own shoe this time, which fortunately missed its mark. A state of frantic dishevelment and agitation had taken ahold of Gail. Her blouse was on backwards, pants missing, my other shoe loosely clinging to one of her feet. I had been gone for less than five minutes.

I navigated the chaos, steering my wife away from various tripping hazards. A broken bone was my primary concern. Eventually, I managed to retrieve the shoe from her vice-like grip and guided her clumsily back to her recliner. Her mood sank together with her deep into the cushions.

After a pause, a sullen breath escaped her. "I have to get out of here."

I called one of the CNAs for backup, a luxury I'd never had at Hunt Club. They were there within a quarter of an hour and with no small effort, gave her an antipsychotic tranquilizing pill. She resisted, irate and frightened. If it wasn't for the adrenaline, I'm sure I would have openly sobbed.

I had mixed feelings about the use of these medications. I believed they were worsening her memory, her communication, and increasing the ever-present risk of falling. But in those unsettling moments, the drugs reduced Gail's hallucinations and severe agitation. What else could I do? I was desperate.

Her mood returned to a sleepier version of this "new normal," and we avoided the need for personal restraints. I felt the weight of not knowing if there was some better way. Oh, how I wished again, and so many times thereafter, that Gail could tell me whether what I was doing was right…or wrong.

By the time the sun peeked through the window that afternoon, my Gail had made another return—sleepy, lucid, smiling at me from the sofa. She allowed me to kiss her. I yearned for so much more than that. I wanted to shower her with affection, to hold her so tight she'd never slip away again. But I knew I couldn't keep her there. That was not up to me. I stayed still in that quiet, sweet moment, trying not to disturb it, like a hiker watching a shy doe enter his path. My little doe stayed with me that evening until she nodded off into a peaceful sleep, and I left her on the sofa until well after dark, glad to let her rest undisturbed.

Just before retiring to bed, the nurses arrived to help Gail change into pajamas and administer her medications. She asked for a hug, and as I did, silent tears escaped my guard. Within a few moments, Gail's breathing grew heavy, mirroring the peaceful rhythm it had that morning, another break in this chaotic world she now resided in. I crawled into my own bed beside hers and fought sleep, not wanting to leave the spell of the previous moment.

I woke suddenly, expecting to check on Gail in the dark as usual, but instead was greeted by a sliver of light shining through the bedroom window. I had slept in, a rare occurrence. It felt good…but only for a moment. Realization that I hadn't helped Gail with any nightly bathroom activity flooded my groggy consciousness—a disaster was likely waiting for me.

Scanning her bed, I found blankets thrown off and only a pajama top covering her. I crept past her sleeping frame and braced for the inevitable mess, searching for missing bottoms, imagining the filthy wake left in every room as Gail wandered in search of the bathroom. An article of clothing caught my attention, an empty pajama leg drawing me to the open bathroom door. I found the missing bottoms lying dejected on the floor—no mess, no smell lifting from them. But an unpleasant odor lingered in the air, and I glanced in the open toilet bowl. A smile of relief crossed my face. She was finally turning a corner, and the proof was floating solid in the water. I couldn't restrain myself from saying aloud, "It is going to be a great day. What a lovely wife I have."

Gail was still sleeping peacefully in her bed, so I cracked open my new journal and began scratching down the events of the previous day. Rarely was there a spare moment to document our journey, but I wasn't complaining. I was in the boat with Gail, clutching the oars tightly as we surrendered to the currents.

"My frame was not hidden from you when I was made in the secret place, when I was woven together in the depths of the earth. Your eyes saw my unformed body; all the days ordained for me were written in your book before one of them came to be." Psalm 139:15-16

Chapter Two

Love and Golf

*Then the sun came out and I decided
the golf course needed me.*

Gail slept through the night again, three nights in a row. No
bed-wetting, just a clean, productive bathroom visit around 2:00
in the morning, then another trot to the toilet at 7:15. Before then,
I had plenty of time to get myself ready, eat my own breakfast in
the dining hall downstairs, and get back to our apartment with her
food before she twitched a wakeful toe.

Gail was quiet at breakfast, a little "far away"—not engaged
with me but not cruel or conspiring, either. All in all, not a bad start
to the day. Her improved appetite and subsiding stomach issues led
to consistent and healthy eating throughout the week. The CNA
came to help Gail dress and make her bed, and later that morning,
we called Gail's mother, Isabelle, at her home in Florida. I never
knew how a phone call or family gathering would go. Gail might
recognize the voice on the other end and smile, participating in the
conversation to the best of her varying ability. Depending on how
she viewed me in the moment, she might also suspect the voice
on the other end to be in league with her nefarious captor. Either
way, I always did my best to translate Gail's mutterings into the

closest approximation of what I thought she meant, always putting them through my filter of positivity for our family. I knew it was difficult for others, especially Gail's mother and our daughter, Darlene, when Gail didn't seem to know them or when she was simply quiet, and there was nothing to translate.

Gail said little during the call, but her mood was good, and it was clear she recognized her mother's fragile voice. Though in her late nineties, Isabelle was chipper and carried the conversation, recalling memories of Gail growing up on their farm in Clinton, Connecticut, on Ferry Dell Road—bathing in the creek and treating the farm animals like they were her true siblings. It was no wonder how much strength Gail had inherited from her mother. When Isabelle mentioned how much Gail loved playing with the little pigs, my beautiful wife giggled and said, "Sure," in a joyful tone. She sat there for at least fifteen minutes, nodding and smiling, making happy chirps and even adding the occasional pleasant "Well!" or "Okay!" These calls did a lot for our difficult days.

The nurses returned around noon for a weekly checkup. Gail's weight was good, climbing back up since her bout with constipation. Blood pressure was 127 over 68—almost perfect and better than most could expect at her age, including myself. Besides the fact that she couldn't remember who I was much of the time, my wife was apparently in next-to-perfect health.

Lunch went just as well as the checkup. She ate every bite on her plate and smiled at me when she finished, saying, "Ready for a nap." After 1:00, the CNA came by to help Gail into her pajamas, and I sat by her as she lay in bed.

A beautiful light filtered through the bedroom window that afternoon—a soft, crisp, late winter light, the kind that pulls at your heart to come outside and feel the coolness brush your skin. I wrinkled my brows and huffed in mock agitation and said, "I'm getting angry, Gail. I want to go out there and play some golf," hoping she'd remember the joke we shared for twenty or so years.

To my delight, she giggled and tried to scrunch her brows back at me, breaking into a smile instead. She placed a hand on my shoulder and said, "You should!"

Her response took me by surprise. I hadn't expected the clear laugh, the kind smile, or the playful mirth felt in her words. But most of all, I hadn't expected this encouragement. On one hand, it pulled me closer to her, not wanting to leave and risk missing any more of these beautiful moments. And on the other, it was only my dear wife who could grant me that permission, that ease of mind and soul.

Golf was not important to me growing up. My young introduction to the sport was carrying bags for members at a club near my childhood home in Madison, Connecticut. After that exposure, I gathered a bag of cheap clubs—tag sale irons here, a hand-me-down putter there—one piece at a time until I constructed a whole mismatched set. But I never really played golf, I played *at* golf on the rare occasion. I never had the time or money for a hobby so demanding of both, until I was much older. I was in my forties, and my daughter, Darlene, came to visit us in Connecticut. By then, it was the late 70s and she was in her early twenties. I remember she was fond of wearing the short shorts of the day, "hotpants" she called them. She came up to me one morning during this particular visit and asked if I still had my old bag of clubs. I did, and she said, "Let's go, then!" I'm not sure what prompted the spontaneity, but it's one of those cherished memories I keep with me fresh, as if it happened just the other day. I played golf that day, blushing red with pride, the prettiest girl in town hanging on my arm. I don't recall what we talked about between strokes, I only know that it was in that beautiful, shared time together that a love was kindled in me for a small white ball and sweeping green hills, a love affair that lasted the rest of my life.

I played whenever I could. During a long stretch of time when I'd lost touch with Darlene, and we didn't have much of a relationship, when I played, it felt like she was there with me, hanging on my arm. Later in life, Darlene had a driver built for me as a birthday gift, professionally fitted to my height and swing. "The way a golf club should be," they told me at the store—a first for me. I'm sure it was worth far more by itself than every other club in my bag. But more than that, to me, it was priceless. Even when I began playing more consistently, I could never bring myself to spend money on a tailored set. But pulling that driver out was like being hugged by my daughter. I swung it as often as I could. Then life changed, and the driver sat in my old bag with its old companions in a dark closet, pushed to the back as other things took priority.

Gail began showing signs of what was to come in 2006, and bit by bit, we had to make hard choices. Moving across the country to be closer to Darlene and her family was one of them, one of the best we ever made. Laying aside golf was another. How in the world could I justify the time away from my wife, when every moment not with her felt like missing a breath while the air was slowly being drained from our lives? We were still alive, but with each passing day, life seemed to slip away a little faster. And the care she needed; I was always going to be the one to make sure she had it. No matter how hard it got, I would never send my wife away to live in a home by herself, surrounded by people who only cared because they were paid to. No one would ever provide for her like I could. The love of a game was no match for the love for my wife.

On that first drive to Victory Centre, however, I couldn't stop my gaze from being drawn by the golf course near the community—the freshly cut tee boxes, the tree-lined fairways, and pristine greens on full display outside my car's window. There was one particular hole that held my attention so much that my driving slowed to a crawl, and it probably took us an extra five minutes to arrive at the Welcome Center. A beautifully landscaped track with picture frame views of still ponds connected by ribbons of water and small walking bridges, all nestled between soft, rolling hills arrested my attention. Every angle looked like a photo out of Golf Magazine. When we finally turned into Victory Centre, I noted how close it was to the course. Entering the main lobby, among the informational papers on the front counter, the words "Golf Lessons" jumped off the top of one page; and right there, filling the rest of the flyer, was an image of the first tee in all its splendor, the same one we had just driven by.

Being so close to Bartlett Hills Golf Course was a prominent selling feature of the retirement community. There were many great features I would come to learn about, but in that moment, I was mostly enamored with one. A great urge resurfaced—the "itch" as many golfers call it—to stride out on that first tee and lace a well-placed drive down the fairway. This wasn't a bother-some itch, but one I had come to love—all the giddy anticipation of knowing you were going to play a round and the joyous relief that followed. The itch grew as I stood there in the lobby, and I repressed the desire to scratch even more. No matter how many perks came with living here, my wife's needs came first. With all that had transpired up to this point, and all I anticipated in the coming transition, the desire to play golf was put in the closet. Time was too precious to be shared.

But things were different at Victory Centre. We lived together, man and wife, in the same apartment; that hadn't changed from Hunt Club. I was a fixture in her life, day in and day out—I was there with her when the sun came up, and I was there to help her into bed when it went down again. But now, I had help. There was no more administering her medications myself, uncertain if she was truly taking them or pretending, staff were present multiple times each day to help us both; no more fearing that she would be taken away from me after her repeated accusations of me running around with other women, as if I was meeting up with them rather than grocery shopping; no more defending myself against her disease-induced paranoia, as though I was trying to poison her or other terrible ideas. With the increased staff presence, those and many other behaviors gradually subsided, and most importantly, her mood and quality of life improved. Whatever was better for her was better for me. All of this added up to a living experience I had not believed possible. The shoe incident notwithstanding, within a few months of moving into our apartment at Victory Centre, Gail hadn't ripped a single button off any of my shirts and never once threatened me with a knife or frying pan. That alone was worth the move.

That little reduction in the constant need to be on guard allowed me to think about other things, and for the first time, I realized just how tired I had become. It's amazing how resilient we can be when we have to be. And for the last several years, I'd had to be more resilient, even with the help of Darlene and others nearby. Many people gave me the clichéd advice I already knew; it was important to have something of my own outside of caring for Gail and responsibilities, a hobby, some pleasure that could take my mind off everything and give me a break from an often-exhausting day-to-day life. I was often reminded by those who cared that if I didn't take heed of my own myriad needs, how could I expect to take on another's?

Darlene keyed in on my stubbly face one visit and told me she hoped I was sleeping more than I was shaving. She would tell me regularly that I needed to think about myself for a change, that it wasn't selfish but a necessity. I had no arguments to offer to the contrary, I just couldn't get myself to feel that way. I realized later, that's one of the main reasons I started journaling in the rare free moments. Writing gave me a reprieve, a pause to reflect, a short break with myself without leaving Gail alone physically. And whenever there was a longer lull in the day, I had something else to keep me occupied.

Scrabble had always been my indoor game of choice, long before Gail's symptoms worsened. It never bored me. Just the opposite; it kept my mind sharp and gave it a better task than worrying or the sad thinking that could creep in. If I was without a Scrabble partner, which was often the case at Victory Centre, Richard played Dick. And yes, each played fair against the other, not using insider knowledge as an advantage. I played when Gail was napping. I would sit at our little table, right in front of the window where the sun streams in. There, I could let my mind wander over word tiles, occasionally looking up to watch people come and go outside. The window was perched directly above the entrance to the community, and seeing people arrive and depart was a form of therapy for me. Sometimes, I could finish a game of Scrabble before Gail called out or showed up unexpectedly, standing right behind me. I think she loved interrupting Scrabble as much as I loved playing it.

But as much as I loved Scrabble, there was something more about golf, some romance about the game, that nothing else could fully replace.

Before long at Victory Centre, I found myself asking other residents whether they had ever played, where they liked to play, and what their handicaps were. Some told me they used to golf but were terrible, and I would smile and remember just how nice it was to play terribly, more enjoyable than doing most other things well. But still, the thought of leaving the apartment long enough for more than a hole or two had never entered the realm of possibility, not until someone decided to give me one more little nudge.

We were in the dining hall for dinner, and I must have been overheard discussing my long-lost pastime with another resident. When my conversation partner had left, and I returned to my meal, I heard a kind voice beside me. "You know you can play... don't you? They give a senior discount."

It was one of the CNAs who regularly came for Gail's checkups. I must have tried to smile through my confusion. Of course, I knew about the discount. But I also knew there was a cost not measured in dollars. I looked at the CNA. She was focused on Gail, who seemed pleased by the attention. The kind woman had one hand placed gently on Gail's shoulder; the other clutched like a treasure by my wife. This woman was radiant with kindness. Her smile lit up the space around us. She turned to me and winked.

"I hear you bothering everybody about golf," she added with a bright and almost mischievous grin. "Every day… like a grounded kid." She laughed, shaking her head. "Why not go? I've seen your clubs collecting dust in that closet. Gail will be fine."

She patted Gail's arm, then suddenly left. I sat there, at first, a little confused, then utterly bothered by the unthinkable notion that I would leave my wife long enough to play golf! That'd be two hours if I only played nine holes. *And who wants to play only half a round?* I huffed in my thoughts as we made our way back up to the apartment. Later that evening, as I got Gail settled into bed, I caught myself laughing about it. "What a thought!" I must have said out loud numerous times. The absurdity both annoyed and tickled my brain while I lay in bed that night. The next day, I woke with the crazy idea still lingering. "I can't," I whispered and threw my blankets off. "There's too much to do."

I got Gail cleaned and ready for breakfast, all the time chiding myself when my mind slipped away to the first tee of a course I'd never played. That morning, I watched Gail eat for more than two hours—quiet, vacant, one tiny bite every few minutes. Besides the sounds of slow chewing, the scraping of utensil on plate, and the plop of the occasional miss, our home was full of silence. It was not uncommon for meals to take at least two hours. *Two hours… two hours…* I slowly mulled over this thought.

The nurses came and checked on Gail, and I found myself ambling around our apartment, studying a space I had so carefully organized for her safety. Gail was soon napping, sitting upright in her chair as she sometimes did. Suddenly, I found that my feet were carrying me down the corridor outside our apartment. A short walk led me to a window down at the end of the hall. The freshly mowed grass outside was covered in the last of the late-morning dew, catching the sun in shimmering glints. I thought about how a white, dimpled ball might fall out of the sky, land upon the damp grass, take one bounce, and then roll to a stop.

During the next week or so, I must have wavered a hundred times as guilt came in waves for even wanting to step away. It was Richard against Dick at the board, and the words each played were even more measured and worth much more.

"She naps much of the time you would be away, and she'd be checked on multiple times by the staff." A valid point made by Dick.

"But not all the time," Richard rebutted.

"Doesn't need to be all the time, though, does it?" Dick countered. "The apartment is safe; you made sure of that. And if anything were to happen, someone would hear. Everyone's in everyone's business all the time here."

"But she would have to wait until someone heard. She doesn't have to when I'm already here."

And that was it. I just couldn't argue with myself when it came to Gail. I wished again that she could counsel me like she had for so many years. But she couldn't. And my own voice would always argue and win for Gail.

One day around that time of wavering, after I had made up my mind, the same CNA—who had kindly urged me into this dilemma of consideration between golf and Gail—showed up in the dining hall and sat beside us; and she just stared at me with a look like I had done something wrong and needed a scolding. "Richard…" she started, shaking her head as a nurturing mother would do a young son. "You're tired. I can see it. You need fresh air. Sunshine. To stretch your legs. And if you happen to do that on a golf course, where's the harm?"

"How can I leave my wife to go have fun?" My words carried a little more attitude than I intended.

"Oh Richard... You wouldn't be leaving her. And you wouldn't be doing it just for yourself. You know that, right?" Her eyes held mine until the point couldn't be escaped.

My head sunk to my chest like a child caught in a fib. It wasn't just the idea of being away from Gail, it was guilt about having fun, enjoying myself. How we often resign ourselves to the idea that a life, especially a spiritual life, ought to be full of sacrifice and martyrdom.

"Your wife needs you healthy, Richard." The CNA's voice was full of loving encouragement. "She needs you to *stay* healthy. You'd be doing it for both of you... but mostly her. I've seen people abandon their loved ones here. That's not you. You care for your wife. No one would ever doubt it, no sir. But it's a long road you're on together. You need to keep up your spirits, whatever it takes. God willing, you'll find just what you need on that golf course. You'll return to your wife ready to be just what she needs." She patted my hand, stood, and left.

It wasn't long after that I was sitting by Gail at her bedside, her soft eyes staring back at me, and the feeling of her joyful words, "You should!" echoed in my mind and heart. She was right, Darlene was right, the CNA was right—I should! I needed to. A tired shell of myself was no good to Gail and no good to me either. I leaned in and gave Gail a gentle kiss on her forehead. "Ok, Gail." Then I walked to my closet and opened the door. For the first time in I don't know how long, I grabbed the handle of my golf bag and moved it out of its dark corner. I gripped it tightly, resolutely. I reached in and pulled out different clubs and irons, feeling their different weights. Then I found the custom driver and smiled.

I wasn't the greatest golfer, never the longest off the tee or closest to the pin. But even then, at almost eighty years old, I could still swing it well, clearing a good two hundred yards or more with my custom-made driver. I was decent with my irons, never long, but consistent. Once on the green, I had a good eye for slope and speed. I didn't use any particular method or complicated process like I'd seen so many friends try over the years. I just felt the shot. I felt a certain balance with a putter in my hand and the ball in front of me that seemed to come from somewhere beyond golf. It bordered on the spiritual, so I never muddied up those moments with anything else. The best result was being there in the first place—just me, the club, the ball, and a stretch of open green. How could I improve on that?

Driving to the course that day, with my golf bag in the backseat and all the hopes of a fresh round in my mind, I felt a happy nervousness and excitement. It was a familiar feeling, like coming home in some way, and I don't think I can explain it any better than that. After paying, I stretched and loosened up, swung a few clubs, then walked up to the first tee box and looked out over the beautiful expanse. I raised my driver, taking everything I felt into one deep breath, then swung, releasing all the tension coiled into my body and mind. I held my swing, and as I watched the small, white ball fly out over the vibrant green grass, every bit of nerves and anxiety released into the blue sky with it. I followed the ball until it landed, bounced once, and rolled to a stop just at the edge of the fairway. I smiled for a moment just watching it sit there, then I stepped away from the tee. As I walked down the fairway, toting my clubs behind on a pull cart, the full glow of golf enveloped me. By the end of the first hole, I rolled in a short putt for an easy par, feeling as if I had never stopped playing, as if nothing had ever changed.

But that wasn't true. A thought tugged at the edges of my mind, and between each stroke, it grew until I could no longer ignore it. By the time I stood behind the ball on the fourth tee box, the glow of the game was fading, crowded by a familiar feeling—guilt. The weight of guilt for forgetting, even for just a moment, that so much *had* changed for us, that Gail was back in our apartment, alone maybe, and that at any time, she might wake up not knowing where she was, why she was alone, or when someone might come to help ease whatever fear her sickness planted inside—that weight was growing heavy. And as I walked to each stroke, I felt my strides slow and my pull on the bag cart weaken.

I have never struggled in golf like I did that day. In any given round, I would have only the occasional duff or whiff or scald of the ball. Not so that day. I struggled in a much more painful way than just a bad round. The entire time, before every swing, I fought the urge to throw the club back in my bag, leave the course, and run back to my Gail. Only the promise of staff, and the belief that God would watch over my wife in my absence, kept me on that course. It was the first time I didn't enjoy playing golf.

Opening the door to our apartment, I set the clubs aside and peeked in to find a flowerpot turned over on the kitchen floor, dirt and leaves and those little fertilizer balls scattered around it. "Gail?" I stepped inside and saw couch pillows strewn about the living room. There was also my stereo, lying on the hard kitchen tiles beside the flowerpot, black plastic pieces and a few buttons strewn around.

She must have gone into a mood when she woke without me there and had free reign to inflict her fears on whatever was at hand. I didn't care about the flowerpot or the stereo.

"Gail?" I called louder and made swift, deliberate steps toward our room.

I found her lying on the bed, looking as calm as I had ever seen. It was as if she had never moved. She looked up at me with those same soft eyes that gave me permission to play, her eyebrows raised questioningly, and in a gentle but sure voice, she simply asked, "Well?"

Suddenly, the worst nine holes I'd ever played were some of the best I'd ever had.

"In this same way, husbands ought to love their wives as their own bodies. He who loves his wife loves himself. After all, no one ever hated their own body, but they feed and care for their body, just as Christ does the church..." Ephesians 5:28-29

Chapter Three

My Job

So, I sit and watch to avoid any serious accident. And right now, Gail is standing next to me, pulling on my hand with this pen, or she'll try to move our coaster chair, or now playing with window curtain and straw shades.

After that first attempt at golf and coming home to find the apartment in disarray, I learned that the CNA scheduled to be with Gail had done her job; she was with my wife nearly the entire time I was away, assisting Gail in the bathroom and getting dressed, then remaining for almost the entire two hours it took me to play nine holes, until the last fifteen minutes or so. That was more than what she was required to do, a testament to the caring nature of staff towards my Gail. But that incident taught me how little time my partner in life needed to cause mischief.

It also showed me that there was little she could get into which would cause her any real harm. If I had to replace a plant every now and again to enjoy the fresh breeze on my face and the sweet feeling of a well-struck golf shot—not to mention the attention to the health of my muscles, heart, and lungs—that would be a small price to pay.

That's just what I did. Over the next several months, I worked golf into the developing rhythm of our life. During that time, Gail's sleep and appetite improved, and she responded more attentively to calls and visits. She seemed to stabilize, if not slightly improve in both her communication and memory, although that could have been my wishful thinking.

My rhythm included the addition of nine holes of golf about twice each week, breaking pattern only for inclement weather or if Gail was struggling more than usual. On any given day, I tended to her needs, helping her freshen up and get dressed. I would set the table for her breakfast, then eagerly anticipate the arrival of the CNA for the morning check-in. On golf days, I would head out for my quick walking half-round, making sure to be back around the time Gail finished her last bite of breakfast. She would be ready for a nap or settled into her favorite chair. This was the majority of our new normal. Golf had restored a piece of me I hadn't realized was missing, and Gail seemed better for it, as if we were a single being sharing each other's energy. I had discovered a newfound ability to give more of myself and be more present, and she began utilizing this immediately.

Around that time, Gail began a new behavior…not so much a mood, as had characterized so many of her changes, but more a state of activity. It came on suddenly. After an ordinary moment, such as breakfast, she would set herself to the task of touching everything within her proximity, feeling each thing purposefully. While doing this, she would talk fluidly in words no one could understand, as though telling someone all about what she was doing. When one area was sufficiently felt and discussed, she would quickly move on to another area, repeating this until she had traveled throughout the entire apartment.

Each of those things, she had always done, ever since her illness robbed her of normal lucidity. But they were always separate activities, and always with less fervor. Something about that phase of our life at Victory Centre had fused those actions into this particular combination that, when in motion, took every bit of energy I could muster to referee.

I came to call it "TTT"—Touch, Talk, and Travel.

The first session came one afternoon after lunch. She'd been picking at her cuticles until one started bleeding. A CD of Giovanni's Christmas music sat on our kitchen counter, a gift from a friend, and I wondered if the soothing piano could bring some calm to both my wife's anxiety and nail beds. As soon as the crisp, clear tones filled the living room, Gail lowered her hands into her lap and became as relaxed as I'd ever seen her when she was not "present". I couldn't believe how well it worked. I'd been told before, music was a key to relaxing many people like Gail, but I had no idea it could work so quickly.

For a solid twenty minutes, she sat quietly rocking, tapping her foot ever so slightly to the beat, looking at nothing in particular in front of her. She wasn't smiling or talking, but she wasn't picking at her fingers either. Then something switched. She began to mutter sounds that were clearly words to her. She wasn't looking at me, but she was absolutely speaking to someone. She stood and walked into the bedroom, then seconds later, came back out with a picture frame she had stolen from the wall over her bed. She walked the frame into the kitchen and placed it in a cupboard, where she proceeded to feel every doorknob and drawer pull. From the cupboard, she collected two plastic cups and transported them to the bathroom countertop under the mirror, all the while carrying on a mumbled discussion. When she appeared again, she was carrying the bathroom hand towel and brought it to the living room, where she placed it flat on her lap and folded it, unfolded it, folded it again, then did that at least five more times, all the while calmly muttering.

"Gail, what are you doing, hon?" I asked. No response.

Now she was done with the towel and headed for the closet, which she opened and produced a picture album of our wedding day. I smiled, hoping this would be the last stop in her travels and might prompt some fond reminiscing. She hadn't located our wedding pictures by herself for years. Today, this book of memories was destined for the bedroom windowsill. The fresh blanket on her bed was to be stripped and folded and unfolded and folded. The pillowcases were peeled and put back on a few times…and so on.

I began hovering behind her like a parent after a two-year-old just learning to walk. I tried to engage her in this sudden new pursuit of hers, pointing out the names of things as she accosted them. "Yes, that's our wedding album. Oh, are you making the bed? Can I help?" I wasn't to be included.

This inaugural episode of TTT lasted a full hour and took another hour for me to reverse Gail's alterations, which included some furniture rearrangement, as well as adjustments of every hanging thing in the apartment and most items in many of the cabinets. I smiled, remembering when a younger Gail had found her love of drawing up house plans and rearranging our furniture each season. One spring day some years ago, I came home from work, exhausted. I droned to our room and plopped down on the bed. Only, there was no bed. Gail had moved it.

A week after TTT began, there had only been one or two afternoons without a session. *New normal*, I thought and smiled weakly after chasing her around for about thirty minutes one day, which included an attempted reorganization of the silverware drawer. This was the first time knives had been involved in TTT…and the first time I intervened with more than an advisory tone.

"No, Gail. Stop, that's dangerous," I said.

She did stop, and afterward, I heard only two connected words within her muttering: "my job."

I turned on Giovanni. Gail sat quietly in her chair, fidgeting but sparing her fingernails, and I sat beside her, resting. The words "my job" were stuck in the front of my mind, and I picked at them anxiously, fidgeting around the recesses of memories as if something meaningful would be found in them. Did Gail think that was her responsibility? Her job? I pictured Gail buzzing around the apartment, her fingers touching every surface, every piece of furniture and fabric. She would stop and pick at the carpet occasionally, bending over with remarkable agility, worrying over some blemish I couldn't see. I'd never seen her so busy, not since…

That was it!

The force of meaning hit me all at once, as if discovering a beloved object from our past in a box in the back of a closet. All our married life, Gail had taken care of our home. That was her job, and she was the CEO, manager, and staff, all in one. First, it was only me she tended to, then our three kids, and then just me again. She cooked, cleaned, and organized our finances and home. She fulfilled all the traditional roles and expectations of a woman from that earlier time, supporting us in every way she could. And she took to this role lovingly, never as if it was expected of her, never resentful. She took pride and joy in her work, and work it certainly was, taking care of me and all the often-thankless tasks behind the scenes. But it was more than just her job; it was who she was. Gail, the woman I love, was a homemaker her entire adult life. She flitted from kitchen to laundry to beds, tidying, cleaning, dusting, cooking, singing…touching, talking, traveling. It was *her job*.

I gazed at my wife as she rocked gently in her chair, plucking at a piece of string worked loose on her pants, and I knew that she was still in there somewhere. She was still trying to take care of things like she always had, still trying to take care of me. I felt her there in that moment. After so much had changed, TTT touched my heart in the way her taking care of me and our family had all those years. Pride for my wife swelled my chest and filled my eyes with tears.

We're warned not to take people for granted. "Cherish the time," they say. "You'll miss it when it's gone."

I never thought I'd done that, taken Gail for granted. Not until that precise moment, when the roles had reversed, and it was she who needed taking care of, did I feel the weight of many missed opportunities to say a simple "thank you," to tell her how much her contribution to our life meant to me. It was time to now. I would show her now how grateful I was for all she had done, and I would follow the example she had been. Proudly and with joy in my heart, I would take on the thankless mantle to care for my Gail as long as she needed me.

During those first few weeks of TTT, I followed Gail around closely, protecting her and our belongings, and in some ways, trying to show her what was and wasn't "allowed." Drawers in the kitchen, for instance—not allowed, along with our few glass, porcelain, or ceramic possessions…and basically anything heavy or with sharp corners. Once my nervousness eased, and I felt settled deeper into this new normal, I spent long stretches just watching her from the living room where I had a decent view of the whole place. I would play Scrabble or write in my journal, or just sit there and stare at my beautiful wife, the woman who could still raise my temperature with a look.

You may find this last phrase strange, especially if you're a young man. I'm happy to be the one to inform you—just because we can no longer carry our wife up the stairs doesn't mean we stop leading her there. We don't suddenly stop being men at a certain age. You could argue, we become the best versions of ourselves in the gentle loving and romantic intimacy with our partners. After all, learning comes from doing, and nothing refines like years of applied experience.

In all our years as man and wife, there was never a time Gail and I didn't have a strong physical connection. Through the difficulties, the children, moves across the country, and even to other countries and back again—through it all, that part of us only grew stronger and sweeter. Every day, she was more irresistible to me, and every chance I could, I showed her that.

Intimacy was one of the first casualties of her decline. First, it was weeks, then months between moments of passion between us. During the early days, I didn't always handle that well. Sometimes I bottled feelings of rejection inside, becoming cold and distant. Sometimes I lashed out in ways I'll always remember with shame. You cannot lead your marriage back to the sanctuary of romantic love through anger. Frustrations must subside and be replaced with tenderness, and that longing must be expressed in patience. If you're not together in this, you don't really have it. Those moments became more and more precious. Gail was still who I wanted to be with, the only woman I ever wanted, and that most intimate and vulnerable way to express love was taken away almost entirely.

As symptoms progressed, and we learned more about Gail's disease, I learned that this was common, and it was unlikely that connection would ever fully return. I needed to rethink what intimacy meant, how to show it, and how to receive it. How we show our love to each other, how often and in what ways, has been part of the ever-changing cycle of new normals. A touch on the cheek or a pat on the back, just a shy smile at the right moment or a sweet word only meant for me—these shows of affection were amplified for me more than any other time in our six decades of marriage.

It's such a cruel irony, now that I think back, that it took losing one aspect of our relationship to heighten the others. If only I had valued all the little moments with the same respect and appreciation, maybe the intimacy of our relationship would have been that much better all along. Maybe the changes and losses wouldn't have hit so hard.

When we arrived at Victory Centre, it had been more than a year since our last "fully" intimate encounter. It was now almost a full year since we had moved from Hunt Club. I had come to terms with that part of our marriage being gone and had begun making adjustments in my expectations along the way. I didn't see Gail as any less desirable, but I would never pressure her, no matter how much I wanted her caress and to hold her as only long-time lovers know just how to. Where I had normally led, I would now let her guide. I would let her show me in whatever way she could what she needed from me and how and when. I was still her husband, and she was my wife, intimately together.

"A wife of noble character, who can find? She is worth far more than rubies. She works with eager hands. She sets about her work vigorously; her arms are strong for her tasks. She watches over the affairs of her household and does not eat the bread of idleness." Proverbs 31

Chapter Four

Family

Then she went and sat on the edge of my bed.
I went and sat next to her. She took my hand. Squeezed it.

"That's Lauren." I pointed to a picture in a plastic sleeve in an album resting on Gail's lap. "Your great-granddaughter. She's four now, but she was three then. Do you remember Lauren?"

"Yes."

She didn't look at me, and I thought there was a slight annoyance in her voice. And no recognition. That happened a lot when we played the "do you remember" game. Sometimes I could tell that she could recall the faces and names, and sometimes she just really wanted to. Other times, it was clear she was confused and frustrated, always signaling the end of the game.

"And who is that, Gail?" I pointed to another picture of Lauren, this one a little older than the previous. Gail's eyes didn't move to the next image, either ignoring me or still struggling over the first picture.

"That's also Lauren," I answered for her, and Gail gave a clear, "I know!" I fought back a laugh. She didn't seem to find any of this funny. While her reactions could sometimes catch me off-guard, in truth, I didn't find much of this comical either. Sometimes, it felt like I was interrogating my wife, or trying to catch her in a fib. I hated that feeling. But the experts emphasized the importance of these kinds of memory activities—in particular, showing her the people she loved and asking her to say their names.

That day, I was not convinced she recognized anyone in the small square images on her lap. I knew she loved her children, grandchildren, and the greats as well. These were immeasurable joys, cherished and unforgettable by the true Gail within. For altered Gail, sometimes those memories seemed right on the surface, ready to be plucked and smiled at with joy-lit eyes, and sometimes they were buried so deep she couldn't recognize her own daughter standing in front of her. It hurt seeing that. I knew it hurt Darlene, although she would never say or show it. She was so strong for her mother and me. I felt, of all the things lost to my wife's condition, the reluctant memory of her family was more my fault than any other.

Gail and I were soulmates from the beginning. A lot of people use that word, and I don't mean it the way most do—an instant and wildly passionate joining, where oceans are crossed to find the one and only connection no other can provide. That's not what a soulmate is to me. I loved Gail from the outset, that much was true, but we had to tend that fire. Every day, we fed it with new fuel, fanning and stoking it so the flames would never burn out. We made the act of loving each other a responsibility and a reward. Our marriage, like any, had its share of problems, but we always came back to that—the dedication necessary to stay married your entire life. And not only to stay married, but to want to stay married…not just "for the kids' sake" or for the image you wish to project—to truly want. That takes careful, intentional tending. It takes a decision from the outset that you are both fully committed to this vision, this shared dream of life together, until death do part.

What we had together, in my mind looking back, would have been difficult to improve. We gave each other our all. I don't regret it. But it's in that dedication to each other where I feel the most regret, with her condition the way it is now. I didn't know it when we were young, nor when the children came into the picture, and not even when we were dragging them with us on mission-focused moves across the country and across oceans. When Gail and I moved with our two boys, leaving Darlene in Illinois with her then boyfriend, now husband, Bill, for the rolling, green hills of Connecticut, I didn't know it then, either. It wasn't until Gail began to slip away that I realized for the first time, all that enduring devotion I had given to my wife, I had in so many ways deprived my children of.

In some ways, perhaps that tended devotion set the tone for how Gail viewed our children. After all, can you have more number ones than one in your life? We can shift our attention and focus to others, but someone or something always takes the primary attention. I had heard some husbands complain that they felt neglected in their marriages, that their children received most of their wife's care. I didn't have that complaint. Also, among many families of our time, children were more ornamental or what simply came with the marital package, better not heard from but just admired. We didn't share that sentiment. But often, we didn't do much better. If they had clothes, a roof, and full bellies, what more did they need? How short-sighted we were, if we knew how much we needed each other beyond the physical, how much more our children needed from us?

But I can't take all the blame for this emotional neglect of the children, as much as I'd like to. After Gail got her driver's license late in life and all the freedom that came with it, it was still rare for her, or me, to make the twenty-minute drive to see our son, Jeff, and his children. Once, long after the kids were grown, Darlene asked Gail from the backseat of the car while we took a drive whether she would still choose to have kids, if she could go back in time and do it all over again. After a pause, she answered a simple "No." I remember the rest of the drive full of silence. My wife cannot explain that answer to us now, but I feel confident that I can answer for her. She did not resent or regret having children. Gail gave our marriage everything she had, and what was left, she gave to Darlene, Carl, and Jeff. But I believe she knew that wasn't enough, long before I knew it myself. Her disease robbed her of her later years and ever making it up to them, but I knew she would have, if only she had been given the time.

Gail and I devoted a significant portion of our early lives to the Church. Sundays were filled with all-day church activities, starting with Sunday School before Worship Service, followed by a meal at home, and returning to church for Evening Service. Throughout the week, our children were involved in various youth programs—Darlene in Pioneer Girls, and Jeff and Carl in the Awana club, which I had helped establish at Pleasant Hill Community Church. Darlene also joined me once a week for choir practice. Very little time was left for just being together as a family. As a man of God, it was my Christian duty to put God above other pursuits.

When Darlene was about five, Gail and I felt a strong call to become missionaries. We moved to Upstate New York to attend the Elohim Bible School, where we would learn the basic customs and language of the German culture and be trained as missionaries. The boys were only toddlers, not yet in grade school, so we brought them with us. Darlene was just old enough for kindergarten, so with a heart filled with a mix of sadness and faith, we made the decision to leave her with her Nana and Grandpa in Clinton, Connecticut. That was a terribly difficult decision, but with so much upheaval, we felt it best for Darlene to have the stability of school and the attention our retired parents could provide. We had faith that we were doing right by God and her.

Later in life, Darlene would tell me that she remembers that year with her grandparents as one of the best from childhood. Her Nana was warm and liked to play, chat, and cuddle, a stark contrast to the tight ship her mother ran. She recalled with laughter how her Grandpa Joe would take her into town for ice cream just so he could sneak into the local store for a small jar of herring and devour it before returning home. This was against Nana's rules, but Darlene, in her own words, "was no snitch." Where they lived in Clinton, the Hammock River ran right up to their property, an ideal playground for a young tomboy like our daughter. Had I known how well she thrived during that year, I might have felt a little less guilt for leaving her behind…and a little more for the next stage in our lives.

After Darlene finished kindergarten, we moved to Germany for mission work, and life was even more immersed in church culture. Gail and I dedicated our entire lives to the kingdom of God. I spent hours each day printing gospel tracts and handing them out on street corners. Gail and I were both involved with church youth camps, me interacting with each season's campers and her working long hours in the kitchen, supporting in whatever way she could. This was our shared mission for God's work. What time and energy we had left was spent with our kids, but almost always with a focus on God and the body of work we were doing for Him.

I fully believed in and was committed to what Gail and I were accomplishing and the positive impact it was having, and I still do. I wanted my children to be a part of that noble work, wanted them to feel the purpose and joy in it. But we were so feverishly caught up in our shared dream, we never considered our children as children, first. Nor did we see them apart from the mission, the church activities, and the treasures we were storing up in the kingdom of Heaven. I never saw their own needs for love and self-development. In our busy tenacity, we weren't treating our children as treasures on Earth.

We had been in Germany for about five years when we felt we had accomplished the work we were called to do there and were ready to move our family back home to Connecticut. I took odd jobs that first year but struggled to find consistent employment in Clinton, and so about six months after returning home, I accepted an offer for work at Tyndale House Publishers in Carol Stream, Illinois. It was about five years later when our love of the lush green, rolling hills and a gentler summer called us back to Connecticut. Our two boys were young teens then. Darlene was seventeen and already an adult beyond her years. She'd had to be, now that I reflect on it. I think it was easy for me to believe that she was better off staying behind, and maybe she was. Looking back, I regret that decision more than most, leaving her in Illinois, not for what happened—she turned out both strong and full of grace, in spite of being left. But what we did for her, what we had always been doing our children's whole lives, was put what we thought we had to do—God's mission, mine and Gail's mission—ahead of them.

When the boys grew up, they made lives for themselves, as children eventually do. Carl moved to Canada and devoted his life to the mission field with the Inuits of Newfoundland. Jeff was never more than thirty minutes away. He still lived in the log home he built when he and his wife were young. He might as well have lived in Canada with his brother, for all the time we spent with him over the years. So immersed in church responsibilities in the time we didn't spend working, we rarely made the time to see them between birthdays and the occasional holiday. I regret that to this day.

Our children had their struggles, each in their own way, with life, with themselves. But I'm proud of all my children. I'm proud of the people they became. I'm proud of who they became because of Gail's and my influence...and despite us. I wish I had spent more time getting to know who they were before they were off and grown and had stayed a bigger part of their lives and their children's lives. I wish I had done that for me, for them, and especially for Gail.

Gail was in her late sixties when the spiral began. The little things came first: forgetting where she had put a spatula or a toothbrush, trouble finding the right words, even small ones, or repeating a question or thought multiple times in a conversation. Soon after, she started forgetting the names of people we interacted with regularly at our church. I chalked this up to the normal quirks of aging. Whether the thought of it being something more ever occurred to me then, I cannot remember. Likely, it didn't, or if it did, I swatted the thought away like a gnat trying to land on my nose. I've always had that ability to dismiss the little nagging doubts. Most of the time, it was a superpower, pushing me beyond what I thought I was capable of. Sometimes, I used it to lift up those in despair. Other times, it clouded my ability to see and acknowledge the reality of situations unfolding.

Could I have intervened earlier in Gail's care if I were less of a glass-half-full personality? At the time, she and I would laugh together over the absurdity of these new "innocent" issues of aging. One day, they were no longer funny. I pulled into our driveway and found Gail standing there next to her little red Toyota car, confused and sobbing, looking at the keys in her hands like she had never seen them before.

Gail didn't have her driver's license as a teen. She wasn't impatient to have it; she didn't need it. Her parents were there to take her where she needed to go, and then she had me. She would sometimes joke that my car was the reason she went out with me in the first place. It wasn't until her mid-50s that she finally decided she wanted that freedom. She enjoyed her new independence immensely, and I enjoyed seeing her with it. She was a woman alive with renewed purpose—visiting those who needed counsel, bringing a meal to someone in need, or helping someone at the church. During the week, she would drive herself to ladies' church, then do the grocery shopping or visit tag sales after. But some days, she would drive with no other aim than to enjoy the dramatic forested hills of Connecticut, the breeze on her face, and boundless freedom on her soul. There was nothing so beautiful as my Gail unburdened, lit up with life.

I smile now picturing the dappled light on her face, the wind in her hair and sunglasses on. One sunny summer day while I was playing golf, she walked out to her car bound for the grocery store…and forgot how to turn the car on. She just couldn't process how to turn the key in the ignition. She panicked in her confusion, and that's how I found her in the driveway. It took some time to soothe her and get an explanation of what had happened. For the first time, the truth was brighter than any amount of denial could shield us from. This beautiful island of life Gail and I had made was sinking into the ocean, and we needed a life raft. I wish it hadn't taken me so long to realize one was there already. She had been in the harbor of our lives, waiting patiently.

Soon after the incident, while Gail was napping peacefully and unaware, I called Darlene in Illinois. It had been thirty-five years since we left our daughter behind. She and Bill had married and built a rich and full life for themselves, complete with two children of their own, Christina and Stephen. Making that call was hard, not just because of what I needed to ask. In the past three decades, we had only maintained occasional contact—birthdays and holidays, mostly—nothing you would call a healthy relationship between parents and their daughter. I knew my grandchildren only from the few visits Darlene and Bill made back to Connecticut and the photos they would send, and they kept me updated on major events. Other than that, I was unaware of their lives. I knew their names, but I couldn't recall their birthdays, and I knew nothing about what made each of them who they were. When I called, I felt great shame in what I was about to ask, and how much of an ask it would be.

After the initial hello and surprise from Darlene hearing from me out of the blue, I asked the question I had called for before I could talk myself out of it.

"What would you say if your mother and I sold our house and moved to Illinois? We'd be closer to you and the kids. Sometime before my birthday this year, maybe?"

There was a long silence, then, "Sell your house? You know Illinois is still brutal in the summer. Mom hates the heat, Dad. And the landscape here is still just as flat as ever. Does she know you're calling?"

I stuttered and stammered, and before I could come up with a response that made any sense, Darlene cut through the nonsense. "What is the real reason, Dad? Is one of you sick?"

I nearly broke down under the weight of that question. Through all the subtle and not-so-subtle signs, I had never once used the word "sick" out loud or silently, not in that way. That was a word reserved for more than head colds and fevers. That was a word for people in true decline, and I was not ready for it.

"Dad?"

"No, no… Nobody's sick," I lied. "We just… There's the grandkids and you and Bill. We miss you, that's all."

I couldn't bring myself to tell my daughter that I was afraid, that I felt like I was standing at the edge of the abyss, everything we stood on crumbling, looking at what the future might hold as things got worse with Gail's dementia, that I couldn't care for her on my own, that I could not see how we could stay in Connecticut, and that I had no one else to turn to. Our church friends were getting older and depended on their own children for help. Our youngest son lived in Happy Valley, Canada, and the other was dealing with many personal issues, and I knew our Darlene was strong, and her husband Bill, the methodical person he was, would watch over us. That gave me small comfort in this moment. Looming before me was the pain of telling my daughter that after thirty-five years of being only a small part of her family at the best of times, we needed to be together as we were about to enter the worst of times. I had taken Gail and my best years and locked us away from them. I had taken that from Gail just as much as I had taken it from my children. I lied to avoid stepping out into that void, and whatever the fallout, I would deal with it when Gail and I were safely in Illinois surrounded by family.

We moved before we even sold our house in Connecticut. With all our possessions in storage, we trekked across the country and moved in with Darlene and Bill. And I braced for the deserved backlash of years of neglect. I stepped into the open air and waited for the crash, but it didn't come. All the anger and resentment I feared Darlene had built up over the absence—all the missed moments getting to know her children, the memories not made, holidays and vacations and backyard get-togethers not attended—she didn't direct any of that at me. There was hesitation at the idea of her mother and me moving in with them so suddenly, but it seemed to last only a moment. Once the shock had passed, she only wanted to move forward. I have no doubt that she felt the vacuum of what could have been, but she was more interested in what still could be. I don't know which would have hurt worse—her righteous anger or the guilt I felt at the undeserved love and support poured out on us.

A sharp knock at the door startled me out of my thoughts. I was back in our living room with the picture album in my lap now, and Gail sitting beside me.

"We're here!" Darlene's voice called from just outside our door.

Gail was still staring at one of the pictures, and I couldn't see any more recognition in her eyes than when we began that day. I felt a pang, knowing the hard moments stayed hard more often than not, and I wished for a few seconds that I could not answer the door, that I could let Gail rest and spare Darlene and the family the pain.

"Dad…?"

But Darlene was stronger than that, and Gail needed this. First and foremost, that was my responsibility now, to help my Gail in every way possible, no matter the difficulty. And she needed her family, whether she knew them or not.

"Coming!" I called back as I slowly lifted myself from our sofa.

Noah and Lauren, our great-grandchildren, were in the doorway beaming their smiles up at me as soon as it opened. Darlene came in after as the innocent chattering began.

"Everything alright?" Darlene asked as she gave me a hug.

"Oh yes," I said. "Just fine. We've been looking at pictures." I walked over to Gail. She was still facing the pictures, but her eyes had turned sideways, taking in the arrivals with suspicion. "Gail, look who came to visit you."

"Hi Gail," said Darlene.

Gail looked toward her and muttered something.

"And it's Noah and Lauren," I added.

"Oh…" she said quietly, without a smile.

"Say hi to your Gramma," said Darlene.

Noah and Lauren walked tentatively to Gail. "Do you want to play with us, Gramma?" asked Noah, holding out the ball they had brought.

Gail looked into her great-grandson's eyes, and her face lit up in a big smile. "Yes!" she said, without any tinge of suspicion.

Something in Noah's voice or in his face, or something we just don't understand yet had caused Gail's light to turn back on, and all at once, we were a family again.

"You're Lauren," said Gail, and Lauren's eyes brightened as she shyly smiled.

"That's right, Gail," said Darlene with enthusiasm.

"There's my daughter," said Gail then, and turned a bright smile to Darlene. I can't remember my heart being fuller than it was just then. I know there are scars that remained from our years of absence, but even in the darkest times, God's shines through us to heal old wounds.

"Catch, Gramma!"

Noah threw the small ball, and everyone cheered as his gramma caught it. Her eyes grew brighter, and without prompting, she tossed the ball back to Noah.

"You're a good thrower," said Noah in his innocent, boyish confidence. "I'll show you how to be as good as me."

Lauren snagged the ball from her brother and took the next turn, and the three of them fell into a game of catch that lasted for several minutes. Little Noah gave Gail tips, and Lauren monitored her brother and Gramma as only a doting firstborn can. After finishing their game of catch, they brought out a small puzzle with ten large pieces and took turns placing them in the right openings. Gail was able to locate several pieces by herself, and with every successful placement, the kids rejoiced with her. It was like that between Gail and her great-grandchildren—no judgment, just playmates spending time together as equals. In that, there was a wisdom we elders have maybe lost touch with in the passing of time—the wisdom in joy and innocence. There they were, just three people that loved each other for exactly who they were without any expectation or fear of change.

Those beautiful little moments, they didn't wash away all the grievances—I had come to learn that's not what healing was. You don't heal by forgetting what hurt you or how you hurt others, but by growing from it. Family had become everything to me, not just Gail or the next mission in caring for her. I know I struggle with a narrow focus and seeing the broader picture at times. I sometimes make light of things to keep positive, while not taking in the full reality. It wouldn't stop hurting that I hadn't been a larger part of my children's lives earlier. But because of that, and all my short-comings, I would spend the rest of our lives tending to and filling in some of those holes.

During the play session, Gail stood abruptly and walked to Darlene. She grabbed her daughter's arm and began pulling her to the door saying, "Walk." I had never seen her single out her daughter like that since the worst of her memory loss set in. I wanted the two of them to have some time alone, so I stayed back to read with the kids.

Gail and Darlene were only gone a few minutes, but that was more than enough to be a very precious gift, or so I hoped. Gail seemed flummoxed when they returned, and I knew that could happen when the scenery changed for her, so I put on some soft music and sat her in her chair. She calmed down, but I worried the visit had become taxing for her, and she might spiral into a behavior I wished to keep the younger kids away from. Darlene must have read my feelings. She told me they had errands they needed to get to and told the kids to hug their Gramma and say their goodbyes. Then she sent them out into the long hall to roll the ball. When we could hear them laughing outside, Darlene smiled and motioned for me to join her in the kitchen.

"She switched in the hall, Dad. Like a light." Darlene snapped her fingers. "Went on about how you bring all sorts of women into the apartment, cheating right in front of her. She says you beat her and shout names at her and starve her. Said she needed my help. She had to escape. I haven't heard her speak so much since Hunt Club."

"You know I would never—" I began out of reflex.

"I know, Dad," said Darlene, and she placed a hand on my shoulder. "I know. I'm so sorry, I just thought, because of the journal, I thought you would want to know. I know you would never do those things. Don't even think it."

I tried to keep the well of tears back, but a few ran down my face.

"I'm just glad Noah and Lauren didn't see," I said, pretending to be braver than I felt.

"Mom loves you. Don't forget that, Dad." And she gave my shoulder a squeeze. "That's not her when she says those things. My mother loves you."

Darlene and I hugged, and then she went over to Gail and got down on her knees in front of her. She gave her mother a long hug and told her she loved her. Gail reached out and played with a lock of Darlene's hair for just a moment and smiled.

After Darlene had left, I was still standing in the kitchen processing what she told me, when I heard my wife's voice. "There's my husband." I turned, and she was smiling at me, and there was no deceit in that smile. My Gail had never been deceitful, nor could she start now. If anything, this disease brought the worst fears to the surface. I knew in my heart that Gail knew me, and I knew Gail, and it was this disease that brought paranoia, fear of neglect, and a waking nightmare of abuse into our relationship. I had to keep those things separate. They were the intruders. My wife's mind had been kidnapped.

"There's my wife." I smiled back and returned to sit next to her.

The next few months passed in familiar rhythms. Some days were better than others, but when family visited, especially when the great-grandchildren were there, Gail's response seemed heightened. During that time, we drove several times to Christina and her husband Sam's place to capture more moments with our grands and greats. Gail became so comfortable at times with Noah and Lauren that she would clap and sing along with their songs, and her great-grandchildren could inspire her to do things no one else could. Time may have been lost with our children, and even their children, but through Gail's condition and in spite of it, we were gaining some of the most precious moments together with three generations of family. And in a strange way, maybe in divine providence, a gift came through tragedy. I didn't want to see my wife suffer with dementia. But it seemed to pull us together. Through this loss, something we may have gone the rest of our lives neglecting was gained. No one could have given me a greater gift than seeing this.

Then one day, when we were firmly and contentedly settled into this new normal, life reached out and threatened to pull that gift away. Gail was waking up from a long nap just before noon when Darlene called. I put her on speakerphone and immediately wished I hadn't.

Noah was in the hospital. He was only three, so full of life and wisdom and wonder…and on his developing brain, a small tumor was threatening to steal it all. The call ended abruptly. Tears ran down my face, and I turned to my wife. She was sitting quietly, staring ahead, no sign of understanding.

I sat down beside her, and we sat lost in the silence.

"Jesus said, 'Let the little children come to me, and do not hinder them, for the kingdom of heaven belongs to such as these.'" Matthew 19:14

Chapter Five
Intimacy

Gail had some tears.
I asked if they were for Noah, she said yes.

The day after the news, Noah's tiny body was scheduled to go under the knife. The cancerous mass was located on his brain stem, and it was aggressive. I wanted to be at the hospital with them but felt it would be a bad idea if something went south with Gail. The family was already going through so much; they didn't need our troubles added on top.

I stayed at our apartment with my wife and thought to myself for the first and only time that I was glad she didn't know what was happening.

I don't remember which Gail was there during those hours, whether she was lucid or tucked behind the veil of dementia. I only remember sitting quietly and staring at my phone and the clock, imagining the fear and pain Darlene and Bill and their children—Noah's parents—Christina and her husband, Sam, must have been feeling.

I was praying when the call came. The operation was successful; the tumor was fully removed. I quietly praised God, then the next words stole my breath. The tumor was confirmed cancerous. Its cells may have already spread to inoperable places within Noah's little body. He would need to begin a six-month-long chemo regimen immediately. The success rate was seventy percent.

Late that evening, I tried to explain the situation to an already fading Gail. I should have waited, but with Darlene doing her best to be strong for her daughter and me trying to support Darlene, I think I just needed someone to talk to. Oh, how I needed my wife then. She didn't understand. I don't think she knew who I was, or who Noah was, or why this strange man was confiding all these sad things to her. She wouldn't take her bedtime medication that night, and she fought her pajamas.

And I snapped.

"Just put them on, Gail!" I shouted. It was just a moment, but the shame lasted long after my outburst. I was so tired and sad, and now angry at myself. I called for the nurses. No one was available at that hour, and Gail was unmanageable for me. I knew I had caused it. My mood and response to her struggle had made her spiral. An angry and confused Gail went to bed fully clothed that night without her medication. I sat beside her bed, then stood and paced outside our room, only to return again and again, not knowing what else to do with myself. When she finally fell asleep, I prayed a tearful prayer that God would be with Noah and the doctors, and all the ladies I loved so much. I asked for strength to be all they needed and to never lose patience with the woman I loved more than anything in the world ever again.

The next morning after getting Gail cleaned and sat down for breakfast, I sat across from her at the table with my hands folded, head down. I couldn't eat that morning, and it was hard to be present with Gail while she ate, so I tried giving up my worries to God once more.

While praying, I realized there were no eating sounds coming from the other end of the table. Gail hadn't picked up her fork. Her hands were palm down on the table. Her eyes were closed. "Love him, Lord… Love him…" She said in a broken voice.

I wiped my own tears away. "Gail, are you praying for Noah?" I asked.

"Yes."

Amen…

Over the next few months, Noah settled into his treatments. The tumor and surgery had robbed him of his speech and most of his motor function. Now the chemo was taking his hair. I gradually came to realize that Noah's situation was affecting Gail. She knew something was wrong; she just didn't know how to process or express it. In the days and weeks after the surgery, we prayed regularly together when she was clear of mind. Most of the time, she sat silently, but when I would mention Noah specifically, she would recognize him in some way—a soft whimper or a catch in her throat. To have her there with me, just in that small way, was more than I could hope for.

Between hospital visits and chemo treatments, gradually, Darlene began to bring Noah and Lauren more regularly to Victory Centre. I was glad to have that time with them and for Gail to interact as much as possible with her great-grandchildren. With the fight both Gail and Noah were enduring, this time together was more important than ever. Their playing together, other than the very real limitations Noah was now suffering, was very much like it had been—no worries or fears, just three people in the moment. Noah struggled to grasp the ball and throw it to his Gramma like he had only a few months before. His mind and sense of humor were still there, and he often found the right puzzle piece but struggled to place it. Lauren, that darling girl, would step in for her brother and her Gramma whenever they needed and cheer for them when they accomplished anything, whether it was her that completed the task or not. These children were just as strong as they were wise beyond their years. I found myself reflecting on the words "Out of the mouths of babes…"

But I could not look at Noah and Gail sitting together without my heart breaking in two—the one half, a joy at seeing our family brought so close together; the other, a pain greater than I thought possible to bear watching the struggle they were going through. I watched Darlene too. There is no love like the love for a grandchild, and I know it took all her strength to stay upright for Christina and the kids. No one would have blamed her for a second if she had broken down. But she never did, not once in front of me or Gail, or the children. I don't know where my family gets their strength. Not from me.

Gail and I were connecting more during those early months of Noah's illness. I won't call it a silver lining; even my optimism has limits. But God must have known how much I needed my wife and allowed her dementia to lift a little. Or maybe she related somehow to what Noah was going through, and it broke through, allowing her moments of rare understanding and empathy. I rationalized these thoughts, but I could never fully know the truth of them. All I knew was that she was more open to communication with me. It felt selfish to me then and still sounds selfish now, taking some amount of joy from a terrible situation. But how can a man not crave a loving word or act from his wife? No matter what causes it, the kindness from a spouse is like water in the desert, and I was parched (or scorched) in the hot, shifting sands.

There were breakthroughs during that time. Gail's therapist had been working with me on the finer points of communicating as a caregiver to Gail, and I was trying every tip she offered. She told me to enunciate as clearly as I could. You can believe, from that moment on, I articulated my words with more effort than at any point in our marriage. Other tricks included keeping phrases short, maintaining eye contact, and finally, using her name each time I spoke to her. The therapist said that one was the most important.

It reminded her who she was, not just for communication but for her overall sense of self. If that went, everything else would go too.

It was awkward at first, saying her name every time I spoke to her. You don't realize how little you say a person's name in normal conversation until you do it intentionally. Instead of "Good morning. Are you hungry? How's that taste? I think I got it right this time," it was "Good morning, Gail. Gail, are you hungry? Gail, how's that taste? I think I got it right, Gail." Short phrases, articulating, eye contact, identification—that was the formula. After only a short time, she responded positively. Fewer sideways glances and dark mutterings filled our days, and she was more present when I communicated with her. I was hooked. What at first felt strained became a gift given to us by her therapist. I saw how it benefited Gail's mood, and that meant more to me than any amount of effort I could give.

Sometime in June of that year, when the weather was beautiful and we were communicating better than we had in months, I decided to chance an afternoon picnic with her down by the Fox River. It was a favorite place of ours before we departed for Connecticut all those years ago, and we had returned there many times during our early years back in Illinois. I had tried bringing her there during the first months at Victory Centre, but could never stay long before she grew overstimulated and overwhelmed. The next outings were only short viewings of the river from the car window.

That day, I was feeling bullish. I led my wife down the hall and out the front door to the car we had taken so many drives together in. I picked up some takeout barbecue, then took the shortest route to the beautiful place we had visited so often. We strolled to a small patch of soft grass under the shade of a large tree stretching its branches over the riverbank. The cool, flowing waters seemed to call us to come dip our feet. This was a spot we knew very well. We had acted like young lovers there once.

Everything began smoothly after we arrived, just long enough to lay out the blanket and open up the takeout bag and start on the contents within. There were no napkins, a nuisance for anyone faced with eating barbecue, but for Gail, sticky fingers could mean an emotional breakdown. No problem, I thought. I tried to show her it was okay to wipe her hands on the blanket. You would have thought I had committed a sin for the outburst that came from my wife. *Richard, you fool!* I thought. Then I reached under my button-up and tore off a piece of white undershirt and gently folded it on her lap, making a show as if we were at a fancy restaurant and I was her waiter, well trained in the etiquette of fine dining. I dabbed the sauce from her face and folded her pretend napkin, once again, on her lap. "Will that be all, my lady?"

Gail was smiling, and I smiled back. The barbecue was agreed to be delicious, as was the pudding I had snuck from the dining hall and the bottle of wine I surprised Gail with after all was eaten. We left the river after a couple hours of eating and drinking, and friendly conversation that consisted of me pointing things out or asking questions. Only this time, responses from Gail were clear and on topic. She was there with me. I wondered if this was what heaven felt like.

After our picnic on the river, I drove Gail to Hunt Club, where we had lived before Victory Centre. Although my mind tended to dwell on the more difficult experiences during the final months of our stay there, we had developed long-lasting relationships with some of the residents and staff. The visit was a spontaneous decision, and I set my expectations low. But here again, Gail surprised me. She recognized many of her former friends and acquaintances. Her characteristic warmth was on display, calling people she remembered by their names and putting her hands on their shoulders or cheeks when she spoke to them. Everyone loved Gail, and there was nothing I loved more than seeing how people responded to my beautiful wife.

After that, I drove us to a small park; the day was too beautiful not to squeeze every moment from it. We strolled along a path beneath trees and through drifts of wildflowers. Gail stopped and smelled many different blooms and pointed at bees and butterflies, laughing joyfully. Even they seemed enamored, buzzing around like doting subjects of my lovely queen.

Eventually, Gail grew tired, and I took her home. An easy supper, meds, and gentle conversation followed before pajamas and bed. After covering her under layers of blankets, I turned to my own bedtime preparations. While brushing my teeth, I thought I heard motion in the bedroom. I leaned out of the bathroom to investigate. Standing in front of her bed was a smiling Gail, no longer wearing the pajamas I had just dressed her in…or anything else.

If you have ever been intimate with a woman—and I don't mean the kind of intimacy that pervades college campuses and hotels near late-night pubs—the intimacy that exists between two people who trust each other so fully that they give each other not only their bodies but every layer of their being. If you've ever experienced that level of intimacy, then you will know what I mean when I say, I found myself in my wife's eyes. Reflecting all we knew of each other, hers were eyes full of invitation…an invitation I joyfully accepted.

Our loving that night didn't consist of hungry groping but gentle caresses. I let my wife lead. This was her boat; I was only there to help navigate the waves.

The next day, I wrestled with what happened. In some ways, I've never fully resolved my feelings about this. Though intimacy was a part of the ever-changing cycle of new normals, it was most often just a touch or a smile, and I had to trust that she was showing me her love in the ways she could. It had been years since we had gone the way of sexual intimacy. That had been a struggle for me, but so was the fear of going that far with her. What if during our lovemaking, suddenly I was no longer her husband Richard but some stranger? Was it right to take that chance? That evening, she had offered her love. And I am still a man—a man who desires his wife.

This was a journey we were still on together—learning, loving, living. I only hoped and prayed that in those few moments, she could feel all of me, all the love and hope and passion. I would never lose that for her.

A few days later, I was sitting with Gail after lunch. Normally, she would have been down for a nap, but that day, we listened to some hymns on CD. "Just a closer walk with Thee…" played on the little stereo, and Gail was humming and muttering some of the words, tapping her foot along with the tune. It was so peaceful, I didn't want to interrupt. Then my phone rang. It was Darlene, and I knew better than to have the phone on speaker this time. I held it up to my ear, and I've never heard so frightening a sound in all my life. My strong Darlene was weeping. Her grief gripped my heart, and the words that followed tore it from my chest.

Noah's cancer had spread into his brain and spinal fluid just one week before starting radiation. There was nothing more they could do. Our little Noah was going home to walk with God. He was only three.

"God is our refuge and strength, an ever-present help in trouble. Therefore we will not fear, though the earth give way, and the mountains fall into the heart of the sea; though its waters roar and foam, and the mountains quake with their surging."
Psalm 46:1-3

Chapter Six
Bright Light in the Sky

It is tough for all of the family, except Gail. I talk about it, but she doesn't understand.

I remember only a few moments from August 25th to the morning of October 3rd of 2015. I kept writing in my daily journal. I know that much. But I never looked back at the entries. I simply couldn't. I think it hurt too much—a period that felt like survival. I guess I just didn't want to relive it. The following is not what I can remember so much as what I just couldn't allow or force myself to forget.

After learning our great-grandson would lose his fight with cancer, every day became a gray, numb struggle. I couldn't hide from the image of his bright face, and always following were the grief-stricken faces of his sister, Lauren, now five, his mother, and grandmother. They were there when I woke each morning and when I lay down at night, and every moment in between. I ached for them in a way that I had never felt before. And that is to say nothing of how I felt for myself—so torn, wanting to break down into a thousand tiny pieces but knowing I had to stay whole for the girls in my life, whom I loved so dearly.

I made a ritual during that time of forcing myself to smile in the mornings before I first turned to look at Gail. If I didn't put on that veneer of bravery before seeing her, I would have no bravery at all. My wife had always fed off my mood, more so in her current condition, though in a different way now. When she was "away," she was like a captive animal, never sure whether she should trust this human caretaker but knowing always that she needed his caretaking. I could not let the frailty of my feelings break through and make her any more reluctant toward me.

So, I smiled and articulated, and said Gail's name. I used short sentences and showed her pictures, and turned away from her every time I saw little Noah among the pages. I did not hide the situation from Gail, only what it was doing to me. When I felt strong enough, I made sure each day to speak Noah's name to her and what was happening to him. I did this in the simplest terms for her sake, and so I could get through what needed to be said. I don't know how much she ever understood. I only know that she began to cling less to me and more to her little white dog, Mickie.

She carried him around, clutched in a one-armed hug, and talked to him as she went about her imaginary tasks. She stroked him as if he were a real pet. I believed she loved Mickie so much because he reminded her of a pet dog we had back in Connecticut, a Bichon, also named Mickie. But during that time, when she scarcely let the tattered white object out of her sight, I wondered if there was more to it.

Though the small canine doll had only just come to her no more than a year before, it looked much older, having been loved hard by Gail. That included her habit of picking at blemishes on the dog's coat, ones only she felt. About half the fur remained untattered. Fur that was once white was now cream, and much of the stitching holding its appendages together was pulled and hanging, or missing altogether. You could say that Gail's stuffed friend was no longer whole, though with every imperfection gained, she only seemed to love stuffed Mickie more. I thought, in some way, this tight bond might have represented her feelings for Noah, that in squeezing Mickie so tight, she was trying to bind her great-grand-son to this world in a way that only she understood. Or if not to the world, at least to her. The more Noah's condition declined and the more I delicately explained, the more Gail held onto Mickie and seemed to need the little doll's presence.

Everything felt like it was happening at once, each little moment of the day stacked on top of the others in a kind of time-less existence. We neither moved forward nor backward. Each day was just the same as the one before—wake, smile, pretend, hurt, sleep, repeat—another day added to the unmoving collage of our current life. That time might have lasted a week or a year. Looking back, it's both easy to believe and heartbreaking to know it was only a little more than a month.

One day stands out amid the fog. Gail and I had been up multi-ple times the night before, once around midnight and again, maybe 2:00 or so in the morning. Bedroom, bathroom, living room—it was a moonlit version of TTT, with very little that was productive happening. She was up to pee, then it was back to bed and fighting to sleep until morning. My pre-day smile came reluctantly.

I stumbled to breakfast downstairs and back with Gail's, then set the table. All went well, despite my lethargy. Later that morn-ing, meds were taken with only a small portion of fuss; good, not great, but we got it done. Then there was lunch and a long nap for Gail afterward, while I attempted to summon enough focus for Scrabble. The letters added up to many words but never the ones floating around in my heart, and I wouldn't have wanted to see those on the board anyway, so I found myself staring out the window instead, watching the people as they came and went, and I stayed put that way for some time.

I was still gazing when Darlene and Bill called. I startled, then hesitated, some part of me wanting to avoid whatever news there was. It didn't matter if it was good or bad. By then, good was only a prolonging of what was to come, an extension of the timeless agony of the present. Bad would only speed us forward to worst.

The news wasn't good or bad. The situation was bad, but the news was just another piece of expected existence. What else was there to expect when a loved one was dying, besides more information about how they were dying?

Darlene and Bill had been staying in Chicago with their children, Noah's parents. They occasionally stayed at the Ronald McDonald House, taking care of Lauren while Christina and Sam were with Noah, and paying visits to the Lurie Children's Hospital where Noah's little body continued to shut down. A decision was made that Noah's time was coming to a close, and he would be transported by ambulance to spend his last days surrounded by loved ones in the comfort of his home. That was the hope, not that there was any reason to doubt his final moments would be best lived in an envelope of familial love, but there was a high probability he would not arrive home in time. For someone clinging so tenuously to life, even an hour-long trip, even in the highest of medical transportation technology, was a high-risk gamble.

But Noah was a fighter. Not only did he survive the journey home but he seemed to benefit from the relocation, if only a small amount. There was no reversal of his prognosis, nothing to make us grasp at such a heartbreaking hope. He just seemed more alive in the light of his own windows than those at the hospital. At least that is what Darlene related to me. I had not been able to break away from my care of Gail to welcome him home. I wonder whether that light was only in her own eyes. That is just who she is. Daddy's girl, I guess.

When that phone call came, it was a week after Noah's return. Darlene and Bill were only calling to confirm if Gail and I were still coming over to see him. I dreaded this, that there would be no light in little Noah's eyes, or so scarce an amount that I would not know him for the boy he was, that he would not know me. I already had so much of that; I didn't know if I had strength enough for more. I feared I wouldn't contain my frailty and be what I needed to be for Gail and our children. Selfishly, I feared that years later, I would remember Noah only as I saw him that day—frail and dying—not as the light he had always been.

I don't remember getting off the phone or getting Gail ready to leave, and I don't remember the drive to Christina's house. I don't remember stepping through the door or hugging the girls. My memory of the visit begins at seeing Noah, a ghost of himself, lying in blankets on the couch, unresponsive, and the singular pain that tore through my heart. Clinically, this tiny angel was still alive. His chest still rose and fell, and his heart still beat, however weakly, but I feared our dear Lord had already taken Noah from this world of suffering. I feared that, and in my braver moments, I may have hoped it. Silently, I said goodbye to Noah that day.

Noah was a hero, the ultimate version of what it meant to be brave. From the beginning to the end of his battle, even when defeat was certain, he continued giving his greatest gift to the world—his light. He embraced every day, always finding the little joys in big and small things. It was as if he already knew the rewards awaiting him in Heaven, free and removed from all the suffering and pain of this world. He was brave, and I was not.

When I saw Noah, I lost control and wept openly in front of my family. I looked at Gail in a reflex of shame, still so conscious of my need to be strong for her. She sat quietly, unaware—unaware that she would soon lose her great-grandson, her little playmate, unaware of my sobbing, unaware of the bright candle among us flickering its last. I want to say that she was blissfully unaware, and I may have felt that at the time, a kind of grief-born jealousy.

She sat there with all of us, stuffed Mickie in her lap, petting and preening it instead of turning her attention to Noah. I don't know if she was aware that he was even there. I wanted badly for her to coo or whimper, or to say a word, anything…for me, for the family, to let us know she was there with us, hurting with us. Gail's body was with us, but she was somewhere else. And that meant I was also in two places, the one I lamented and the other I couldn't see. Neither place I understood.

After being perfectly still for a while, Noah made a movement, just a subtle twitch, nothing any of us would have noticed in any other situation. Gail turned her head toward him and in a quiet voice she said, "Oh." I don't know if Noah heard his great-grandmother, but we all did.

If the previous month had been a dim blur, the next several days were a dark void. We must have staggered our way through those motions that make a person continue to live, but that is all I know. Sometime during the void, Noah's body became aware that its animating soul had departed, and with no purpose left, it ceased functioning and came to that eternal rest.

The morning of the funeral, I rose early and choked back violent tears in the shower until my ribs hurt. I thought it best to get what I could out and be strong for Gail until better moments allowed me to grieve more.

Gail was easy that morning, and I thanked the Lord for that. The CNA helped with meds and applied some lipstick and color to her face. She was congenial while I drove her to the funeral, her eyes smiling and turning this way and that, taking in the scenery like a child leaving home for vacation.

When we arrived at the funeral, I avoided the receiving line which stretched out the door of the church, down the steps, and into the parking lot. I told myself this bypass was for Gail who would struggle to stand that long, and that was not a lie. But it wasn't the whole truth. Darlene sat on a small stool in the vestibule of the church receiving condolences, and that was more than I could bear at the moment. An empty seat rested beside her. I later learned Bill planned to occupy it and had tried to, but he had to remove himself, too. It had been too much for even him. I could never blame him for that. I understood. How often it's implied that we men are the strong ones…but I believe it's more often our women who carry the heavy emotional burdens we are too afraid or weak to carry.

I guided Gail past the line directly to Darlene. I fought tears as I briefly hugged my daughter. So many pictures of Noah surrounded her. Darlene hugged her mother, and Gail smiled like they were meeting for nothing more important than afternoon tea. Her attention turned to the photos of Noah, and she oohed, and her smile deepened. Another day, I would have delighted in this recognition.

I choked down the grief-stricken spasms in my throat and chest as I guided my shuffling wife away from the receiving line, quickly past Christina, Sam, and Lauren, and into the sanctuary to our seats on the second row. Small packs of Skittles awaited each of us—Noah's favorite candy. Gail settled into her seat and was quiet, a behavior reinforced by decades of church attendance. It felt like there was only Gail, me, and Noah's small white casket there at the front of the sanctuary. He felt close enough to touch and simultaneously an endless distance away. After what seemed an eternity, the last of the attendees found their seats, and the funeral proceedings began.

I don't remember much of the ceremony, who spoke, in what order, or what they said. When the video of Noah's short life was played, I heard the background music, but I confess, I saw few of the pictures through the tears. And when my eyes were not blurry, my limited focus was split—the majority spent maintaining my composure, the rest afforded to the awareness of Gail. If her mood turned south, I would need to remove her swiftly, and that took constant vigilance. One moment during the eulogy, I do remember clearly. I felt my breath leave me when Sam, Noah's father, told of how Noah had undergone not only three surgeries but, in 181 days of treatment, five rounds of chemotherapy, numerous spinal taps, MRI's, CT scans, central line dressing changes, and blood and platelet transfusions.

When these horrifying statistics were uttered, I remember turning to Gail instinctively, forgetting just for a moment and expecting to find my wife of old sitting there, ready to anguish with me at all we had just learned of Noah's last days in life. But she had not heard these agonizing descriptions. This was my wife of now, the current new normal. She was smiling like a child. She didn't even look back at me. Throughout the service, her mood teetered between quiet and detached, and bordering on glee when the music played. She would tap her hands and smile, and shift in her seat while I tried ignoring the varying looks from those around us who didn't understand. I don't believe Gail ever noticed the small white casket just a few feet in front of her tapping feet.

At the end of the service, 1,263 balloons dropped from a net in the rafters of the sanctuary, one for each day of Noah's life. They were green, his favorite color. Many children were in the audience, some who knew Noah, others who did not. When the balloons dropped, they squealed in delight, unaware, as children often are. Gail's reaction was the same. She giggled and clapped, and when she reached for a balloon that drifted near us, it was her first overt reaction since we had arrived. After the funeral, children sifted eagerly through baskets of toy trucks belonging to Noah, choosing their favorites. It was clear Gail wanted one, but I chose not to lead her in that direction.

In the evening, Team Noah, comprised of approximately one hundred close family and friends, participated in a 5K run to raise awareness and funds for the fight against childhood brain tumors. It was sleeting and cold outside, and some of those present remembered how, while most avoided weather like this, Noah would have delighted in the chilly magic of it—his joyful delight immune to the cold discomfort, only taking in the dazzling reflections. After the run, the team shared stories of Noah's shortened but remarkable days of life. They lit lanterns to remember his light, though none of them shined as brightly as he did. I only knew of these events that occurred, listening to the relating of their tearful details from loved ones.

That night, I was in our apartment with Gail, sitting quietly, surviving the feelings of the day. Suddenly gripped and consumed by grief, I found myself angry that Gail wasn't truly there with me; and just as swiftly as I succumbed to these feelings, I hated myself for feeling them. I thought about the parallels between Gail and Noah, each taken by a vicious disease, each suffering the ups and downs of its whims. But I ended that line of thinking, afraid to go where those thoughts might bring me.

Noah Samuel Willis; Born April 13th, 2012;
Departed September 27th, 2015.

He blessed us with his light for a little while.
We will remember it forever.

"He will wipe away every tear from their eyes, and death shall be no more, neither shall there be mourning, nor crying, nor pain anymore, for the former things have passed away."
Revelation 21:4

Chapter Seven
Hand in Hand, We Walk

In the case of dementia, the game of marriage is over.
Now the vows become real.

After Noah's funeral, time seemed to begin counting again, and the world continued turning. When I woke the next morning, I felt like it was a new day, not just a repetition of the same painful existence. The pain had not decreased. No magical switch had been flipped to change how much I felt the loss. That would never fully go away. But there was something about the funeral being past that allowed the family to begin healing together. I have been tempted to call it closure, but it feels wrong when I think about it that way. Once Noah was declared terminal, we weren't waiting around for him to be buried. The truth is, I think some of us were waiting for a miracle, and none came. Instead, Noah transformed when he left his body. He took on his true form. Unhindered by his mortal vessel, he became for all of us an eternal and boundless version of what he had always been: a light to unite us. With him no longer suffering in pain, maybe we could start the process of learning how to live with ours. That might be the true miracle.

"A part of us is in Heaven now," Darlene shared with me once as we were sitting outside by the pool at her home.

I nodded and smiled, reflecting on what she meant as I stared at the rippling light reflecting on still water.

"You made me," she continued, thoughtfully. "And I made Christina. We are in Noah, and now he is with God."

I nodded again, then looked at her. I saw in her eyes the same comfort I felt at the thought of being there with him in that small way. I could always count on Darlene to know exactly what to say in hard times.

In the days and months that followed, I often wondered whether Gail could feel Noah's absence or if she felt his presence in heaven.

In the wake of Noah's funeral, I noticed a few drops of blood in the toilet after Gail had peed. I always checked the contents, feeling partly like a thief or pervert sneaking a peek at my wife's private business. But when someone can't faithfully tell you how they feel, you must be willing to cross certain boundaries to gain the information.

"Are you feeling well, Gail?" I asked, hoping for a moment of clarity.

A mumbled response followed, which I took to mean, "No, and I don't care for you looking at my pee."

Sorry, dear.

Her mood was subdued on the way to, during, and after church, and there was blood again after a noon bathroom visit. I called and asked the CNA to check her out, and she was there within an hour with an answer.

"This has been building," she said. "She's going to need anti-biotics, ASAP."

I don't know whether the CNA was scolding me as she said this or whether it was the guilt I felt making it seem that way. It was clear the infection had been many days in the making, and Gail would have been in increasing pain during them. My attention had been occupied between my family's pain after losing Noah and my own. But even in that, I felt ashamed I hadn't been more observant. If you've cared for an infant or a beloved pet, you may have some idea of how I felt. I was a terrible caretaker. A fit caretaker wouldn't let their wife suffer. Then I wondered what other pains she might be enduring, and in her way was pleading with me, yet I was dumb to her cries.

I took Gail by the hand, leaving the CNA right there in the apartment, and drove straight to the emergency room. We were at the hospital for three hours, three hours which I spent torturing myself. When we were finally called back, I apologized to the nurse for not catching this sooner, that I would do better, I promised. I turned to Gail and made the same promise.

The nurse smiled at me with concerned pity, like I was the injured one, which rather than a comfort only frustrated me further.

"Don't beat yourself up," she said. "Your wife will be fine. Honestly, with people in her condition, these things aren't usually caught this quickly. You did good. She just needs some antibiotics."

Medication was administered immediately. Gail was just as subdued as she had been, and I was still upset as we were sent back to our car with a week's regimen of pills. The nurse's words had only shifted the direction of my frustration. I would rather it *had* been my fault; at least that was something I had the power to fix—I could pay better attention in the future or enlist more help. But the nurse had painted a picture outside of my control, one where Gail was simply doomed to suffer with these situations until the symptoms were long-endured and obvious.

As I reached to open the car door for my wife, she patted my face and smiled at me, and a large portion of my immediate angst melted away. She giggled as I helped her into the passenger seat, and just like that, the terrible danger vanished, and a spell was cast—Gail was my hot date on a Friday night so many years ago, and I was her strong beau. As if we'd been transported back to our innocent youth, I knew things weren't all that bad. Everything would work itself out.

In my sudden euphoria, I pulled out of the hospital parking lot and took us for a shake and a burger. She squealed when we pulled up to the drive-in, and my heart skipped with the melody in it. She was right there with me, returned from that mysterious place her mind had disappeared to. Like two kids, I talked, she nodded and smiled, and I was so wrapped up in my girl, I forgot all about my food while she finished every bit of hers.

Gail was wonderful that night, putting on her pajamas and taking her meds without fuss. After she was in bed, I sat for a few minutes alone with my journal, wondering with a buzzing mind what had caused the sudden change. Had it been the antibiotics, a relief from pain freeing her into an elevated mood? Maybe it was as simple as the trip to the hospital, a stimulation to reignite her personality. Or maybe it was a break from the clouds that had settled in our apartment after Noah's passing. I noted those things and said a silent prayer of thanks that I'd caught the situation and there was a remedy. With effort, I shifted my focus to the morning. Tomorrow was Sunday, and I would give my final sermon for the residents of Victory Centre.

I was an ordained minister with years of service in the Church, which I felt best allowed me to be of use to each community we were a part of. Upon arriving at Victory Centre, I immediately felt called to bring words of hope to my fellow residents, many of whom lived with so very little. The idea was well received, and I began the very next Sunday, speaking to a group of around ten. It grew over the months, and soon there were around twenty of us enjoying each other's company and finding comfort in the words and wisdom of our Lord. But after a time, what had been a calling became a weight.

Most people don't realize how much time it takes to prepare a message, even a short one of fifteen or twenty minutes. When you are the primary caregiver for a person that requires constant vigilance and aid during the days, the hours it takes to craft coherent words have to come at times when your mind is least coherent. I would do most of the prep work during the week then finalize my sermon on the weekend. That usually fell to Saturday evenings when Gail was asleep, and the apartment was quiet.

Sunday mornings after service, I would be greeted with remarks like, "That was such a wonderful message, but are you sure you're doing alright?" or "Gail looked so beautiful following along with the music and watching you speak. How do you find the time?" Then, there were the more direct words from my family… "You don't look good, Dad. I think you need to start prioritizing yourself a little more."

Those were Darlene's words, of course, and not new ones. Variations of the sentiment had started some months back and were a constant companion anytime she visited. As time passed, she told me I was looking more and more tired, and she went so far as to dissuade me from Sunday morning services and all the prep they required. She wasn't wrong. She rarely was. I would drop a responsibility and gain some much-needed time to rest. But she didn't seem to understand just how much that time spent meant to the other residents or me.

A few weeks before Gail's infection, Darlene and Bill were over, and they had "sat me down" for a talk. I always knew when I was about to be sat down. Darlene had a look reserved just for those moments. She would say "Dad…" in a way that in one word meant, "Dad, there's something you need to know, and you're not going to like it, but I'm going to say it anyway, so you'd better sit down."

I did.

"We're just concerned," said Bill. "You look frail and tired… I don't think you realize how tired you look."

It was the same message that had been repeated for the last several months. I sat and nodded, agreeing visibly and disagreeing silently, as I had each time before. I wasn't going to change. The one-sided conversation had gone on about the usual length that I would wait until making my rebuttal about how much people need hope and how there was no one else here to give it to them.

Then I coughed.

It was a rattling, wet cough, and it wasn't my first of the day. I'd been coughing like that all week and had yet to get it checked out. Then Darlene said something she had not said before.

"Dad, when you get sick and land in the hospital, then what? What happens to Mom?"

I was suddenly aware of just how tired I felt. Realizations came in rapid succession—how little I'd been sleeping, how often I didn't eat, my appetite gone after spending hours attempting to get Gail to finish her own plate, that three or four days would pass without taking a shower because I didn't have the energy left after another fourteen-hour day of caregiving.

I nodded to what they were saying for the first time without the intention of ignoring their advice and continuing on with my business. I would think about them. I was unable to stop thinking about them. I would look at Gail sitting in her chair and picture a world where I was not there. It was not an easy decision, but in this light, it had become an obvious one. My sole purpose on this earth was to give Gail the best remaining years I could, and that would be impossible if I wasn't around. This boat of ours was still sailing against turbulent weather, riding low in the waves, and I had brought extra weight aboard. It was time to lighten the load before I sank us.

The urinary tract infection arriving right before my last Sunday preaching served as a sort of confirmation that it was okay, that I had made the right decision. Fortunately, I had built a relationship with the head pastor of Village Church in Bartlett, a place Gail and

I attended occasionally. They provided a pianist to play on Sunday mornings at Victory Centre. I met with the pastor when I decided to end leading sermons, and he graciously offered once again to fill the void. They would send pastoral staff to meet this crucial necessity for our residents.

I continued sitting and thinking that night before my final Sunday preaching, and the more I thought, the more I realized the move away from late Saturday nights and early Sunday mornings was overdue. It wasn't just the tiredness and the recent cough. Gail had also started some new behaviors that I didn't care for. Several weeks before, maybe months, I noticed her walk had changed, a sort of hitch in each step or a bit of hesitancy, like a person trying to avoid stepping on bugs that littered the floor.

"Gail, are you alright?" I asked, the first time I observed this. Mumbles.

She wasn't showing any signs of pain that I could tell, but the change was noteworthy. Over time, I noticed her pause before stepping was more pronounced in certain situations, like stepping down from one stair to the next or anytime there was a change from one walking surface to another, like tile to carpet or grass to sidewalk.

Additionally, during this period, her sitting down also slowed. When she approached a chair, there was more than the usual slow, assisted descent into the cushion. First was a glance, then a positioning, then another glance, the way a pup circles a spot before laying down. She would do this several times, then begin to lower, only to raise and glance again one last time. I would encourage her that it was ok, but she would glare at me, glance again, before finally plopping down in her chair as if taking a leap of faith.

I brought this to the attention of staff and was told that this was common among dementia sufferers, but it was not a good sign. Gail was losing her depth perception. This could be a temporary condition, one that comes and goes, or it could be the beginning of a permanent worsening. Only time would tell. One thing was certain: leaving my Sunday morning responsibilities behind had been put off too long.

The next several months were filled with high peaks and the deepest, shadow-filled valleys. Every good day, one in which Gail would eat well and seem to be lucid and present at times, was followed by a week of bad ones. The high I'd felt that afternoon leaving the hospital with antibiotics and enjoying our drive-in date was like a long-forgotten dream. Gail had always walked with one hand in mine or on my arm, but now that was a requirement, not a sign of endearment.

Her cognition was also suffering, worse when she was "away," but noticeable when she was lucid as well. She no longer recognized her toothbrush or our apartment door, or which shoes were hers. It wasn't only her depth perception that seemed to be suffering but her vision altogether. The only thing she seemed to never lose a connection to was Mickie, her stuffed dog. Even that relationship had lost some of its luster. Where before she would coo and stroke Mickie's head, now she held him blankly, a tenuous grip on his sparse coat.

There were many days during that time when Gail said no words at all, just sat and rocked in her motionless chair. She wouldn't speak to me, not kindly or because of previously shown paranoia. She didn't seem to be aware of me or anyone else, even the invisible visitors to whom she had given so many words in the past. She seemed as close as one could come to being comatose without being in a coma.

Her situation got so bad that the CNAs, and then the doctors, took notice of this changed behavior. For the first time, that dreaded word I had heard so many times directed at others was spoken to me. I wasn't ready to hear it. I knew this was one of those situations a person could never really be "ready" for; they could only hope it never came, and if or when it did, try not to let it break them.

"We strongly recommend you begin thinking about this, Richard," our doctor suggested. "Discuss it with your family. We're here to help in any way we can. I know this is a difficult decision."

Hospice…

"Truly I tell you, whatever you did for one of the least of these brothers and sisters of mine, you did for me." Matthew 25:40

Chapter Eight

It Takes a Community

It's 6:30 and still no CNA. I changed Gail, cleaned her,
put pajamas on and helped with meds. 7:15 to bed – too late.
I'll do my best for the woman I love.

In the midst of Gail's deteriorating sight, depth perception, and balance, we celebrated our 60th wedding anniversary. During the times of change in her illness, it was always difficult, wondering when the symptoms would stop growing worse, and we could settle into another new normal. Going through that and trying to push all the fear and frustration down to celebrate your relationship with the very person on whom your fear rests, I'd never been so torn in different directions with emotions.

But on that day, March 24th, 2016, I would bend all my energy to making Gail feel that my love had not faded, and our marriage was enduring. I woke her with a kiss and led her through her morning routine of bathroom, clean up, and to the table for breakfast. She ate well, and then the CNA came, but she was not alone. With her was a hair stylist I'd arranged to give Gail an in-home hairdo. Her face lit up when the stylist told her she was going to make Gail beautiful.

"Me?" Gail smiled.

"That's right," said the stylist.

I smiled at the CNA, who already knew the rest of my plan. In as much haste as I could conjure at nearly eighty years old, I kissed my bride of six decades and was out in the hall, bound for the car. I phoned the bakery on my walk and was told the cake would be ready when I arrived in seven minutes—a classic yellow with custard and strawberry filling, with frosted buttercream, Gail's favorite. Next, I arrived at the wine shop where the clerk helped me select a lovely Asti Spumante, with creamy little bubbles and aromas of honeysuckle and peach. Lastly, because I couldn't have them wilting before they brightened Gail's arm, I stopped in at the florist and collected a custom corsage of pink and white carnations with purple statice and purple ribbons to match. Arriving just in time, I watched the hair stylist show my beaming Gail a mirror. I snuck past and delivered the stealth package to the fridge where they would sit for the next few hours.

Lunch was easy, and I wondered if it was just the elation of the day or had Gail made the trip from our apartment to the dining hall with more confidence than she had recently? After eating, we returned to our apartment and listened to a collection of songs from different chapters of our life. I began to pull out the picture album but thought about the potential frustration it could cause Gail because of a lack of recognition or perhaps evoking sadness with pictures of Noah, so I put it away. Gail was napping in her chair when I came back into the room, and that was just fine, maybe ideal. A little rest could be very helpful for what was to come next.

At 3:15 that afternoon, I woke Gail with a gentle hand on her shoulder. I pulled the flowers from behind my back, and she squealed and gestured to herself.

"Yes, Gail. They're for you," I said. "For our 60th wedding anniversary party."

I thought she might never stop smiling, and indeed, she didn't for the rest of that evening. We went down to the cafeteria, where a group of staff and residents waited for us, the cake already set up on the table, bubbles ready to pour. I don't remember any particular words anyone said, just lots of congratulations and hugs, and outpourings of love. I remember how I felt—honored, full, warm. I felt like the luckiest man alive to have my beautiful bride of sixty years hanging on my arm. I remember Gail's smile, brighter than the fluorescent bulbs of that room, more vibrant than the flowers she wore. In a time of difficulty, there was no darkness strong enough to quench that light.

The only dark spot in the day, if you could even call it that, was when I used Gail's nap and the subsequent activity of the afternoon as my opportunity to retire stuffed Mickie. It was beyond worn, so threadbare it couldn't be washed without copious amounts of the tufted strings of its coat coming out. I was worried about the unhygienic implications of Gail's contact with it. Like a child, she often put it up against her face or kissed it, even sometimes mouthed it like she was teething. I felt awful stuffing Mickie behind my golf clubs in the closet, a place I knew she would never look, but I was doing it for her own good. I placed him in his dark rest and thanked the stuffed dog for his tireless service. We were in bed by 7 pm after a very eventful and joy-filled day, and we were both asleep within minutes.

There was one other less than enjoyable moment that night, coming at bedtime when the CNA was supposed to deliver Gail's medication…and didn't. When I called and asked if they would be coming, they said they were busy taking care of other residents and I would have to administer it myself that night. I knew there would be times when that was unavoidable. Victory Centre suffered from a constant trickle of turnover at the CNA position and regularly had to make do with temp help. These workers weren't familiar with the individual needs of residents and often overlooked things they might have seen as simple or unnecessary. Most of the time, they would apologize and take ownership for these situations.

The person at the other end of the line that night didn't sound sorry. In fact, they sounded as though it was me, the person who was paying them for help, that should be sorry, that my request for them to do their own job was the problem. By simply asking for help, I was made to feel like the villain. This had become a part of a larger pattern over a few months. It wasn't every staff member, and it wasn't all the time, but it was often enough that I had grown weary of it.

I've been known to point out a fault or two in my life, and I've faced some backlash. Darlene was always quick to correct me when I would say things like, "Your face is going to freeze that way" to a frowning individual, or sometimes to a smoker, "You aren't the one smoking, the cigarette is. You're just the sucker." I didn't intend to make light of people's circumstances; I wanted to point out what I thought they needed to look closer at. But once we moved into a facility where our quality of life so deeply depended on the goodwill of others, I became aware just how damaging those comments could be.

That was their business, and frankly, I wasn't perfect either. If someone was letting their bad day bleed into everyone else's, I'd usually try to ignore their behavior, politely, or at the most, try to give them a bit of encouragement. Never was I more tested in being a silent observer than at Victory Centre. Keeping thoughts to myself wasn't the difficulty. The moods and behaviors of others had begun to affect the boat, and that made their business my business.

Gail and I were already being battered this way and that by things outside of our control. Adding to this a palpable energy of irritation from the people you relied on every day threatened to capsize us. Most help did not have this affliction, this need to inflict their misery upon others. Most were kind and mature enough not to spread a sour attitude, even if they had things to feel sour about. Most came into our home and smiled or at the very least, simply went about the tasks needed and made a quick exit without displaying their disdain. But a select few seemed to take whatever difficult situation was going on at their own home or whatever drama existed in the staff lounge, and even whatever negative belief they cultivated within their own minds, and allowed that to permeate their care of Gail. That's where I drew the line. I simply could not allow someone else's problems to become Gail's.

To a large degree, I was not without empathy for their circumstances. I was not a stranger to being overworked and underpaid, which was no doubt the situation most people in that building were in. Add to that situation, being short-staffed and doing a job that is difficult at the best of times, and I had plenty of reasons to be patient. But if they lost their patience with my Gail, then I would not maintain my own. There are just some things that call us to be the absolute best version of ourselves, and that is when the life of another is in your hands. If you can't uphold that line of integrity, then you should not be in the business of caring for others. This was a problem with one CNA in particular. She was pleasant at first meeting, but over time, little things began to make an appearance in her care—a huff here, an eye-roll there, and one day, it escalated.

"What the *hell*, Gail?" I heard from our bedroom. The CNA was helping Gail into her pajamas, and apparently Gail wasn't being as cooperative as the CNA would like. I stopped what I was doing in the kitchen and joined to see if I could help. The situation deescalated, but it was not without tension, and I could see that Gail felt it too, contributing to a challenging morning as Gail's mood tended to spiral on days that didn't begin well. I asked the CNA if she was okay, that she seemed a little on edge, to which I received both the huff and eye-roll that was becoming normal, with no words as she left.

It wasn't long after that the same CNA had come to assist in cleaning Gail up after a messy night. This time, I positioned myself in the kitchen but was only pretending to occupy myself so I could listen closely. In a hushed tone, I heard, "Gail, I swear to God, if you don't get in this *f—ing* shower right now…" and then a pair of grunts, one from the CNA and the other unmistakably from my wife.

My face flushed from a calm, ambient temperature to an intense boil in the few seconds it took me to move between the kitchen and bathroom.

"Leave. Now," I said firmly. "You are not welcome in this apartment or near my wife again."

My voice was calm and unyielding in the same way a dam holds back a giant reservoir of water. The CNA did not test my structural integrity, and I'm glad for that. If you asked my family, they would tell you I'm a peaks and valleys kind of guy. My natural state is to ride the contours of my emotions throughout my day. But those high contour lines tend to be happy, joyful, excited ones, rarely anger and even more rarely anything like rage. Since taking on my wife's care, I put a lot of effort into shaving off the highest heights of those peaks and pushing the contents of them down the hill to fill up the valleys. I understood that what our boat needed was a more even keel. That morning, I was not on a peak; I was the peak itself, volcanic and overdue.

When the young lady had left, I was still steaming. I had to leave the room for a brief spell before I could return to comfort my wife, clean her up, and prepare her for the day. I felt exhausted after the short exchange, like it wasn't the beginning of the morning but the end of a long day at the end of a long week. When weekends provide little rest and nights have you waking every few hours for joint trips to the bathroom or to check on the status of bedclothes, you have less patience for the shortcomings of others, and the need for peace becomes that much more important.

But even so, the morning's event also left me feeling ashamed and even a little weak-minded, not because of my reaction to the CNA—that behavior was inexcusable no matter the reason. But in the moments after I witnessed examples of sour behavior, I found myself dwelling on all the other rotten behaviors exhibited by the staff and residents alike. I battered them all with thoughts of "ungrateful, childish, immature, lazy people. All they do is complain…" And there it was, me complaining about other people complaining, a realization that I was swept up in the distorted cycle of thinking, which altered my view of others. Where was my compassion and grace? This negative view wasn't me. That wasn't true to who I am. I was a helper, a giver, a person who stepped into difficult situations and did what I could to make them better. If all these people were frustrated with their situation, me blustering about it wasn't going to help anything, and it was likely to do the opposite.

That day, I made it a point to thank every member of staff I passed. It was easy and authentic, once I made the decision. The truth was, they *were* doing a difficult job, but it didn't have to be a thankless one. I made a point to smile and greet each resident I came across; maybe their day would be brightened with the warmth of another if they weren't receiving that from anyone else. This was not new to me. I'd always seen myself as that person to lift others up; I'd just let my own gratefulness begin to dim amid the noise.

"I just wanted to tell you how thankful I am for what you do," I said to one CNA. "I know how difficult this place can be, and you make all our lives better every day."

His smile was so big, it changed the temperature of the room.

"Thank you," he said, and then something else happened that I was unprepared for. "How's your golf game lately, Mr. Sonnichsen?" he asked, and I could tell he really wanted to know.

It was the first time he had said more than five words together to me in the whole time we lived at Victory Centre.

"Great," I said, then added something about a bad game of golf being better than a great day doing anything else, and he laughed.

He was still beaming as he walked the other way down the hallway that led to the dining room, and so was I walking toward our apartment and Gail.

I chatted away to her when I arrived, and it seemed the mood was infectious. She smiled and said a string of words that were mostly jumbled but ended in a clear "lovely."

I was on a high again but not the destructive kind. I felt lifted above the din of chaos and turmoil, free in a way I didn't realize I needed—to be true to myself like I hadn't fully been since Gail's condition had worsened.

A decision was made then, maybe not with spoken words or even thoughts, but in the form of intention that grows in the heart and spreads through your being to become part of who you are… or a return to who you always were. There was nothing impossible if my thoughts and actions reflected the very love and graciousness poured out on me daily by God. Perhaps that was how God granted miracles, through the loving acts of people placed in our lives? Who knows, maybe even the CNA with a negative outlook and harsh demeanor could be softened.

That evening, a CNA was helping Gail with her pajamas and medicine, and I found myself in the kitchen listening, even after my decision to be more loving and gracious, fighting the urge to become worried. It was a CNA I hadn't yet expressed my gratefulness toward, and I wished I had stopped her as she came in, but old age and the newness of the intention had robbed me of the thought. I heard a soft voice from the bedroom, something like a whimper, and I felt my heart rise in my chest. *Not again*, I closed my eyes and prepared to intercept…then was stopped.

The whimper was actually singing. This CNA was softly singing to my Gail. I stepped quietly to the entrance of the bedroom, not wanting to disturb the beautiful moment. I listened to the whole song, and by the time it was over, Gail was asleep. The CNA tucked her in, stood and turned, then startled at my presence.

I mouthed an apology, and she smiled and waved it off. We stepped into the living room, where she told me that singing brought her comfort, and she loved giving that to others. Before she left, she turned and said that some of the staff members had mentioned how good they felt being thanked by me.

"You're one of the good ones, Mr. Sonnichsen," she said, and then she squeezed my shoulder and left.

"Anxiety in a man's heart weighs him down, but a good word makes him glad." Proverbs 12:25

Chapter Nine

Many Hands

Saw the doctor. Says significant decline in speech
communication and motor. Things are not the same.

It was the kind of decision that seemed to have no winners, the kind that forced you to choose between evils competing to be the greater.

"I know this is a difficult decision," the doctor had said.

Thanks, Doc. Hospice wasn't a difficult decision; it was an impossible one. It's the kind of situation that seems to choose for you, but one you try to put off for as long as possible.

Gail was on what felt like the longest downward trend since the onset of her symptoms. Her diminished sight, balance, and depth perception had led to two falls—one in which she sustained a gash on her forehead, the other, thankfully just a short slide to the floor, after which Gail looked around amused that she was suddenly sitting rather than standing.

I knew those instances were recent, but I feared they were signals of what might become less rare, and I was sufficiently shaken that my golf outings or leaving the apartment for any reason required careful planning of visits in intervals from staff and family. This was a burden they assured me they were willing to accept, to give us as much normalcy as they could, but one I knew they felt, nonetheless. I limited my departures to the shortest length and spaced them out as far as possible.

After a week spent entirely within the walls of our domicile and after coming to the end of my coughing episodes, I took a small window of opportunity to visit Darlene and Bill's backyard swimming pool, sans clothes.

I wouldn't say I was a regular skinny dipper, either in my youth or during the slow fading of my behavioral filter that every person benefits from with increased age, but when I had the rare chance and inkling, there were few activities that allowed me to feel freer than a refreshing dip in the buff. My daughter's back-yard had privacy enough, and if any neighbors happened to see an old man next-door wearing nothing but the suit God gave him, well… I suppose they'd have a right to complain. None ever did, or I never heard about it from Darlene. In any event, I thought the change in scenery and clothing might unclutter my mind enough to arrive at the pressing decision more clearly.

It was a late spring day, and the water was a few degrees colder than I would have liked, but that only added to the reset I hoped for. As I drifted around the pool on my back—something I could do effortlessly and for long spells, a result of my time in the Navy—I allowed a dozen or so circumstances from the last several months to float to the surface of my mind. Gail had tripped over the line in the floor between the bottom of the stairs and the short hallway that led to the dining hall, nearly dragging both of us to the ground. There was no change in the floor's height to cause this stumble, only the perception in her mind interpreting the distance incor-rectly. The long days seemed to come more often now, sometimes two and three in a row, when she wouldn't so much as look or speak to me or anyone else; and that far-off look she wore during these episodes, like someone lost in the woods, unable to see their way out. The inability to find her fork or spoon at times during meals was a new one, too; I had to either be patient and encourage her to eat for hours or feed her every bit myself. And most concerning of all was her drop in weight; it was dropping rapidly.

Hospice can't fix any of this. This is just a part of the journey. We'll soon reach a plateau and ease into another new normal. I'm still enough for her...aren't I?

The word "hospice" had always brought to mind the image of "dying." And the two ideas had become synonymous to me. To apply for hospice felt like a betrayal toward my wife, my commitment to be all she needed. Hospice felt like I was giving up. But when I quieted these anxious thoughts, I also knew hospice represented the increased help we both needed. I was only one person, after all, and one declining with his own age-related issues. I wanted to give my Gail every chance at a happy life, especially in our last years, especially in this struggle she endured. But even so, this decision felt like a spilling out of all the blood in my heart.

It didn't matter how I looked at the situation, how cool the water was, or how little clothes I was wearing, I couldn't see hospice as anything other than a service to help people die easier. My wife wasn't dying; she was just sick.

"Discuss it with your family," the doctor had also advised.

That's a swell idea, I thought as I toweled off and dressed. They would be home soon, and if there was anyone I could count on for an unbiased opinion on why hospice was out of the question, it was Bill, Darlene's husband. A career airline pilot, he was as linear of a thinker as I had ever known. I don't think bias even existed within him, much less as a thing to use.

He and Darlene arrived home and were surprised I was still there, until I told them why.

"Oh, Dad, I'm glad you stayed," said Darlene.

The visits away from Victory Centre had slowed with Gail's new symptoms, and I knew the family was eager to see me healthy and clear-eyed.

"Bill and I have been discussing hospice also," she added.

I was caught off guard, and they could tell. In the few minutes I had left to spend, they took rapid-fire turns explaining to me that hospice was actually a whole suite of services to help aged people with serious illnesses, people like Gail, that it was about her and my comfort…not about the end. It was a service for the living. I was there listening, but my mind was walking for the door as soon as Darlene first said the word "hospice." My body soon followed, and all the words they spoke as I made my exit felt like little darts hitting me in the back as I ran.

A CNA had been helping a distant Gail get cleaned up after breakfast when I left that morning, and when I returned less than two hours later, they were just leaving. Gail had napped and was up again, sitting in her chair.

"She's had a good morning," said the CNA. "No fuss. Not much of anything," she smiled consolingly, "but she seems content."

After the CNA left, I sat beside Gail, and she didn't look over, just continued staring straight ahead. I leaned back fully into my seat and stared ahead, too, at nothing in particular. I was not lost in thought; I was avoiding thought. I looked back at Gail, then back at nothing on the wall, then closed my eyes for a time.

I might have dozed off. I only know that I was jolted back to the present when I sneezed, loudly—the kind of sneeze that had always drawn Gail's ire, the kind that came on so quickly that the body could only produce the most instinctually available response, a cursory attempt to block the expulsion with a free hand. I had a fleeting thought that the chilly dip might not have been the best idea.

"You need to wash your hands," said Gail.

I could have almost missed it—the words that were just spoken—so casually, so matter-of-factly, so exactly like Gail, words I'd heard for decades. I turned, and my wife was looking at me with clear Gail eyes and a clear Gail smirk on her lips. The next words weren't said, but I heard them just as clearly: "I wish you would sneeze into your arm."

I nodded and walked to the bathroom to wash my hands and to remove myself from Gail's sight before she could see me crying. These were the times I missed the most, the ones that might have annoyed me before. "If I had time to blow into my arm, I would have," I would have normally shot back in response to her reaction. A few minutes' silence would follow…or we might have bickered. If we were both at our best, we would have laughed it off, realizing what we had always known, that we were both human, and humans needed grace. But now, her small scoldings needed no patience from me. And just like that, my tightly held hesitations about hospice relented.

She had a good morning… That's what the CNA had said. I had been gone, and she'd had a good morning in the care of another. The result was one of the best moments we'd had in weeks. Maybe my Gail also needed a little time away from the norm, as did I. And such moments like these were a chance for her to be herself, if only for a few seconds. I didn't know how many weeks or months or years we had left. But if I could give her the space she needed, no matter what that service was called, I should.

With the help of Darlene, Bill, and the staff at Victory Centre, we applied and were approved for hospice care for Gail.

Within days, they were there, and the effects were immediate. They offered a level of care I hadn't realized we needed. Social worker and chaplain visits were provided for both of us, together and individually, a music therapist to engage with Gail and coax her into participation in words of encouragement, routine check-ups for weight, sores, or bruising due to falls, medication monitoring and adjustments, in-home care visits catered to Gail's specific needs, and most importantly, the ability to call their nurses all hours of the day and night were to be a part of our new normal.

They even established a schedule with the CNAs of Victory Centre for nighttime visits.

I didn't sleep any better during that first night of hospice care, worried they wouldn't show or that they would show and not know what to do. I tossed and turned and was still awake when the door clicked open at 10:58 PM. Quiet steps made their way through the apartment and into the bedroom, where they found Gail, quietly lifted her blankets and assessed the situation, then left. That was the easy one, I thought. The real show began in the dark of the early morning.

I must have fallen into a shallow sleep, because the turning of the knob woke me again just before 2 AM. The same nurse, I noticed, and again, not a word. The same check ensued, only this time, she gently guided Gail up, escorted her to the bathroom and back a few groggy moments later. "Hmph," I might have let out. *Too quick,* I thought, *probably an easy one, or they didn't clean her up all the way.*

When the nurse left, I got out of bed to finish the job. I lifted the blankets, sniffed, and was met with no odor. Gail didn't even stir, as though she had fallen back asleep the moment her head rejoined her pillow. I laid back down and tried to recall how Gail had eaten that day, whether she was having a "light" night or whether she was just saving her best for last.

I woke with a start that morning, light filling the room to announce that I had overslept. My head popped up, scanning the situation. My worst nightmare—Gail was not in bed. *Where? The kitchen? The bathroom?* I jumped out of bed and found her sitting calmly in her chair.

"Gail?" I said, stumbling over my feet to stand before her. "Are you ok?" I scanned the room and attempted to notice any unwelcome smells coming from any of the various directions they might originate. There were none.

"Sleepy," is all she said. I realized she was not telling me that *she* was sleepy but remarking on *my* having slept in. She had a delightful glimmer in her eye; this was no scolding.

I stood there a moment in awe. I took notice that there had been several turnings of the pages on the paper calendar which hung on our kitchen wall since the last time Gail was this alert before breakfast. This was only morning number one of hospice care, and I wished I had relented sooner.

"Hungry," said Gail.

Coming right up.

"Trust in the Lord with all your heart, and do not lean on your own understanding. In all your ways acknowledge him, and he will make straight your paths." Proverbs 3:5-6

Chapter Ten

Longest Day in Years

What a weird day. Just sitting. We actually danced a little.
Not a fun day, but Gail has been very good. This has been
the longest day in years and years.

"Get out," said Gail.

While getting used to our new normal surrounding the additional support of hospice care, which included better sleep for me and an improvement in Gail's mood and communication, I also had to accept the return of negative moments. With the higher highs came the lower lows. In the past week, she had invited her imaginary friends back into our home, started a somewhat clumsier version of TTT, and often struggled with my increased attempts to interact with her. This was a letdown at first; some unreasonable part of me hoped she would lead in the direction of the wife I knew, not the one I was always relearning.

But with this new normal, I was thankful for its most important benefit—Gail was more active, more alert, and more present than she had been in months. If that meant a few dark stares or out-of-the-blue commands that I leave our apartment, I would take it.

So, I followed her orders and got out. I stepped into the hallway and began the first of several laps around our wing of the building. It wasn't the first time, and part of me wondered if Gail knew she wasn't just sending me "away" but into rigorous and necessary training.

For the past few weeks, I'd used the few gaps in each day to walk the corridors. I'd sometimes carry 2.5-pound dumbbells to increase the difficulty while Hip Hop and Rap music jammed in my earphones. Yes, believe me when I say I loved a good beat. Later that morning, all the training would be put to the test during the Alzheimer's Walk. Over fifteen hundred people had signed up to walk a total of three miles in support of finding a cure.

I didn't compete the year before and was inspired by the team that had shown up to raise awareness for pediatric brain cancer after Noah's funeral. When the Alzheimer's Walk flyer found its way to the front desk of Victory Centre, I signed up that very day and began conditioning. Although Alzheimer's is only one of the many forms of dementia and not Gail's specific affliction, it was more common than it should be for residents to succumb to the disease and be moved to a memory care facility.

I felt nervous at the starting line, waiting anxiously for the race to begin. The person beside me wore a confident smile and seemed ready to conquer the course with ease. It had been a long time since I participated in anything like a competition. Golf was a competition against oneself. When golf went well, there was often no one there to gush over you, something that I disliked. And when golf didn't turn out the way you wished, you could return to your car and wipe the round from your day, you being the only one the wiser. But today there appeared to be far more people than I had anticipated, as though an entire football stadium was crowded into a small block of downtown Calumet.

The gun was fired before I was mentally ready. I stumbled into my first few steps but quickly found my rhythm and focused on a simple pace. There was a lot of jostling about during the first hundred feet or so, no small part caused by this being a group of mostly seniors on senior legs and senior hips, but also because there were just so many of us. We shook out of our early compaction, and the flights began taking shape.

To my surprise, I found myself near the front, in the group of "serious walkers". To my greater surprise, I stayed there. My training had paid off, it seemed, and so much that this felt as much like a "nice walk" as it did a race…for the first 1.5 miles when I hit the proverbial wall of my physical limitations. My lungs started burning, and my legs began to feel a little less sure. I felt a stitch in my side and was reminded of much younger days running longer distances for my school or during summers when I scampered about with friends. The fatigue came so suddenly, like my body knew exactly the distance it wanted to do and was now shutting things down. I had to force my legs onward to maintain my place with the serious walkers, a place I had by then decided I belonged, whether I actually did or not.

I heaved in gulps of air and hurled them back out, desperately attempting to keep up with oxygen demands my body had not experienced in quite some time. Then it hit me. I hadn't played more than nine holes of golf in several years, which from the senior tees, was nearly 1.5 miles. I reasoned with myself that I could still play eighteen holes without any issues. And when I had that thought firmly planted in my mind, my body believed me.

As quickly as the difficulty had come, so did it leave, like a bag of weights cast aside. During all the self-convincing, I'd unknowingly walked the next three-quarters of a mile. I was coming quickly to the end; just a few more blocks of downtown, and I'd be there. Ahead of me were only a few members of the serious-walkers group I'd found myself a part of.

I pushed on, putting in the same effort I'd had when I overcame the difficult stretch to this much easier portion we were in, and I found additional speed in my legs. I passed a walker. Another block behind me and two more walkers passed. One more to go, and the finish line neared. I pressed hard on the gas and threw myself into the last stretch…and finished first.

For my participation, I received a shirt, a bag of Walk to End Alzheimer's memorabilia, and a first-place medal that I hung on the back of our apartment door, more as a way to introduce the topic in conversations than boasting. But more importantly, I helped raise around $2,000 for Alzheimer's research. There was something very meaningful and healing about being a member of such a community, cemented together by a common struggle. The Alzheimer's walk was a highlight of my year and a thing I don't think I could have considered doing were it not for the uptick in Gail's health in the caring hands of the hospice team and the encouragement from family.

Not long after this beautiful event, I took another walk, though much shorter, but one which threatened to have considerably greater impacts on me and my life with Gail, one that has lived on just as viscerally in my memory.

With the increased stamina I'd gained from the Alzheimer's walk, I began taking Gail on the same walks I'd used for training to get her out of the apartment, to greet fellow residents, and keep up my physical routine. I pushed her in a wheelchair and spent twice the amount of time for a solo walk, due to the need to stop every half minute to return a dragging foot or grasping hand back within the boundaries of her vehicle. But I was happy to do this for the benefit of exercise and hopefully for Gail, the regular change in scenery and contact with people other than our few visitors.

It was October 12th, 2016, a day I'll never forget—I was called unexpectedly into the Victory Centre Administrator's office to chat. For what, I did not know. The administrator, Vicki, and I were friendly, and I had enjoyed our interactions, seldom as they were. I must admit, I didn't enjoy them that day. Soon after a little small-talk, she cleared her throat and informed me that I had been accused of physically battering Gail, that I had been seen by a staff member slapping Gail's arm "violently" while wheeling her through the halls. I would not be told the name of the witness.

I didn't need to be.

The day before, I had passed her in the hall, the same CNA whose words and temperament toward Gail had caused me to banish her from our apartment, the same I had reported to management, the same I had attempted to be kind to in the aftermath, and the same I had smiled at in the hall that day and greeted with a kind "hello." A dark smirk was received in return.

I couldn't imagine what difficulties had existed in the past of this young woman to create such a lack of warmth and empathy toward others. I felt as sorry for whatever the circumstances of her life had been as I was angry at her for inflicting them on my wife and me. But more so, I was shocked, demoralized, and emotionally crushed as an individual, a caretaker, and a man.

I was informed that Darlene would be called and that, most likely, a police report would have to be filed. Then Vicki said the two words that stung the worst: "against me".

Against me... A report would be filed against me!

"Until it is deemed that Gail's safety is no longer compromised," Vicki went on, "we'll need to remove you from her apartment."

I couldn't bring my brain to understand this existence I found myself in. I was seen as a danger to my wife.

"Against me?" I mumbled.

"What was that?" Mr. Sonnichsen.

I don't remember the rest of that conversation, whether I tried to plead my case or sat there dumbly. All I remember was leaving Vicki's office and calling Darlene. To her, I broke down emotionally in a jumble of words and feelings which all added up to the same thing—I was going to lose Gail, and Gail was going to lose me. I don't know which of those scared me more.

Darlene calmed me down like only she had the ability to, and it was only then I realized I hadn't even told her what happened. Of course, I hadn't slapped Gail's arm or any other part of her when she would grab the handrails while I pushed her. I was careful and kind. I explained to Darlene the walks we would go on, reminded her of our strained relationship with the CNA, of whom I'd already confided in her about many times before, and then broke down again sobbing.

Darlene assured me she would call management and do whatever was possible to resolve the situation. Time being of the essence, our call ended abruptly. I felt as alone as I have ever felt, heart pounding and paranoia setting in that police would arrive any moment and tell me I could never see my wife again. I shook with fear and anger—all of this due to a moment of revenge and callous spite.

Who will stay by her side twenty-four hours each day and be there when she cries out in the night? Who will be her advocate? Who will read between the lines of her mannerisms to know that she is hungry, scared, in pain? Only I knew her that well. Only I could calm her in the worst moments. They were going to take that away from her. This boat we were on together was being threatened by another kind of storm, not built up by disease but one I felt just as helpless to do anything about.

Those were the worst twenty-four hours I can remember. Within an hour of getting off the phone with Darlene, she called me back and let me know that she was encouraged by her call with Vicki, that the police weren't going to be called just yet, but that Vicki wanted to sit with me again and get my full account of the story.

It wasn't until the next day that I was able to meet with her, but I was allowed to return to my apartment. That gave me reason to hope that there was a chance this would all be behind us soon. I walked through the door and saw Gail smiling in her chair, a CNA sitting beside her, and I had a moment of pain thinking I was going to be under surveillance with my wife, but the CNA smiled and squeezed my arm before she left, a silent assurance that I had more than Darlene in my corner. I prayed that night that there would be at least one more.

I never fell asleep. I was tossed back and forth between all the what-ifs. What if they decided I had been abusive? Would I be allowed to stay at Victory Centre in separate living arrangements, only to have contact with my wife under supervision? Would it be worse than that? Would I be tried for battery, tossed in jail at eighty years old? Gail did not seem to know anything unusual was happening, like a child unaware of the turmoil the adults were going through, and I was glad for it. Those were the rare fleeting moments I appreciated parts of her condition, but the moment would flitter away, and I would have thrown myself in jail if it meant she were returned to her full self.

The next day, I met with Vicki, and the tone was decidedly different than before. Darlene had made an impression on her. She was warm and kind and understanding. She listened to my account, and I believe I saw some shared understanding in her reaction to my explanation of the history between me and this troubled CNA. Vicki nodded to the details I gave, as though reliving her own memories of this particular staff person. Something I related to Vicki must have gotten through to her on a personal level as well. At one point in our conversation, we were both in tears as she related to me that she wished every caretaker was as dedicated to their loved ones as I was. She had seen so many come and go, and it was only the rare few who showed a love that was truly unconditional.

"You understand, that's why we have to pursue any complaint or accusation, don't you?" Vicki explained. "So many residents, especially those who cannot communicate for themselves, are at risk of being taken advantage of…or abused. Sadly, by the ones who are supposed to love them the most."

My fears calmed as I better understood the position she had been put in by the accusation. I had compassion for the tough job she managed.

Before I left, Vicki told me she was comfortable putting this situation behind us, and the police would not be involved. I thanked her, and I apologized, not for anything I had done but for the simple fact that this was a situation she had to deal with. I reiterated to Vicki what I had already said many weeks before.

"Vicki, I'll never let her near my wife again. Never."

Vicki nodded, and I left to be with my wife.

I don't know if it was because of my conversation with Vicki, the situation as a whole, or if something had already been in the works, but I only saw that CNA for about a week after the event transpired. I was glad she was gone, but there was also a sadness left in the wake, like I had failed in some regard toward her as a person I simply couldn't get through to. I thought ill of the situation and never had closure with it. I don't think of any person as being beyond help; there is no circumstance greater than the love of God. I hope she found that. I like to believe that maybe someone reached through her pain and that her hurts are healed.

"Love your enemies, do good to those who hate you, bless those who curse you, pray for those who mistreat you." Luke 6:27-28

Chapter Eleven
Words for the Soul

Yep, Gail will wake up and want to get in on the fun. She'll
wander over and reach out to grab a few letters, tilt the table,
toss something she has in her hand on the table…
It's her way of saying, me too.

Life was decidedly better at Victory Centre without the darkened presence of the angry CNA. Life was better; Gail was not.

With the ever-steady presence of the hospice workers, Gail's health and mood seemed steadier but not improved. There stretched a period of several months with very little muttering, scowling, or accusing me of various imagined things, like cavorting around with other women. That was a relief. What wasn't a relief was her becoming more and more subdued—fewer bouts of TTT, and when they came, they were short bursts, followed by sitting in her chair staring at her hands, the floor, or off into some distance beyond the apartment, quiet and confused. Her speech came only in garbles and slurs. Less often were the single-word responses or short sentences that visited out of the blue.

I know I burdened my daughter during that time with worries about Gail's decline and desperation for some way to slow it. Darlene spent time on her computer searching for the answers. I don't know if that was because she wanted to or to appease her frantic father, but she was always there when I needed her. Like the rest of the medical community, she never found the cure, but she did find information.

We learned that there were many forms of dementia, each affecting different parts of the brain and in different ways. Alzheimer's, we learned, was a very specific form that matched some of the symptoms Gail was experiencing. Then there was FTD, or Frontotemporal Dementia, which matched most of them.

Gail was never diagnosed with FTD. By the time the symptoms were all present, she didn't need to be.

The research pointed to a grim future for Gail. Frontotemporal Dementia shrinks the frontal and temporal lobes of the brain. Those are the ones associated with personality, behavior, language, memory, and cognition. Behavior and language suffer first. Then come hallucinations, compulsive behavior, such as tapping and lack of judgment, loss of inhibition, decline in hygiene, delusions, and eventually, the sufferer begins to have trouble swallowing, becomes perpetually unsteady, and loses virtually all ability to communicate. Essentially, my wife would continue to lose all remaining vestiges of herself and her quality of life, and then she would die.

Darlene visited more around that time, late in 2016. Sometimes she brought Bill or Lauren, or both. Other times she would come alone, just to sit and talk with me and us, often separately. I needed that. I needed the time to just sit with my eldest child, apart from Gail. In some ways, I felt like a parent needing time and conversation with another adult, but one who knows, really knows, what you are going through. In other ways, I just needed someone else to see and acknowledge me. We would talk about many things— Gail's health, my health, staff issues. If Bill was there, he would chat with us for a time, then invariably find something broken to fix in the apartment. And when my daughter and I were alone, the conversation would always begin the same way.

"How are you, Dad?" She always knew the answer and also knew I was better for being asked.

Then I would tell the version of the truth that I needed to tell. "Doing ok, sweetie. We have everything we need, and I truly believe these are the best days of our marriage."

I didn't always feel it when I said it. Sometimes I did, and always, I wanted to. I hope that does not make me a liar. I don't think it does. Even when I didn't feel those were Gail and my best days, I believed they were. I truly did, in a way that I could not have understood without having gone through it myself. It wasn't because Gail had changed. I didn't magically and against all logic love her more when she lost her ability to communicate with me in words. I learned how to love her better. I learned how to let go, to do all that I could to make things better, but to otherwise give the results to God and the ocean he had us rowing through. For maybe the first time in our marriage, I released my expectations of my wife, completely; and in doing so, I didn't just release her from them but freed myself from those expectations as well.

It has been said by many that expectations are the thief of joy. I would add to that they are also the thief of relationship and love. How can you give your full love to a person you hope will change?

I don't know if I ever communicated that well to Darlene. She would ask what I meant, and I would just tell her how I felt, and she wouldn't press me. Sometimes I would forget how hard this was on her, the daughter of my wife. I could go a long time seeing myself as the victim of this story, but that was never true. During that stretch of regression for Gail, one of the most consistent symptoms was her inability to recognize those she loved the most, and this, I knew, was deeply painful for Darlene.

For nearly two years by that time, my daughter had joined me in calling Gail by her name only, never using "mother" or "mom" to help Gail keep her grip on her identity. But I wonder if that very act also hastened her loss of connection to who her family was. If she was no longer "mom", then Darlene was no longer "daughter." Whether that was part of the cause, the result was certain. Gail rarely recognized Darlene, Bill, or any of her children and grand-children. Her tether to Lauren as her great-granddaughter seemed to stay the longest. When she was present, Gail brightened as she always did, and when I asked if she knew who Lauren was, she would always nod or mumble something I took for "yes."

Darlene visited several times in December of that year, and with each visit, I could see the little ripples of pain beneath the calm surface of her face. She would walk through the door and say "hello" to no acknowledgement from her mother or try to chat with her a little while feeding her spoonfuls of lunch and receive no words and only avoiding eyes. One day, Darlene called Jeff during a visit, and there seemed to be some small recognition. Gail stood from her chair and walked over to where Darlene held the phone, smiling. She reached for it, and Darlene handed it over, both of us smiling in shock toward one another. But only a few minutes into the conversation, it was apparent that what we had taken for some understanding of the voice on the other end was more likely an innocent interest in the phone itself, like a new object of mystery to a child.

For these reasons, I was both greatly looking forward to and dreading Christmas. The morning of, I knocked and waved from my window to each staff person as they arrived. There had been an uptick in mistakes, not uncommon for the holiday season as everyone has their minds on pumpkin pie and Christmas presents, and I knew also that this was a particularly difficult time to be away from family. So in my small way, I would remind them that they were thought about, needed, and valued.

They would look up and squint at my antics, then break into smiles at my goofy grin staring back at them. If I saw just a few of them step a little lighter into our building, that was enough for me to face my own day.

Christine and Sam stopped by for about thirty minutes that morning, or so it seemed—visits from family were never long enough. They dropped off a card and some treats for Gail and me. As she always did, Gail glowed and mumbled sweetly at Lauren. And Lauren, the amazing child that she is, held her great-grand-mother's hands and led her around the apartment, chatting with her, then sitting with her until they left. This was also the Christmas that Lauren gifted her grandma a baby doll. This was one of the best gifts Gail ever received. Each day, she loved it like it was a real child. She would change it, kiss it and coo, and carry it around the apartment with her. This was a great replacement for Mickie, and it also seemed to fulfill some need of hers to mother.

About an hour after the grands and great grands left, Darlene, Bill, and Stephen were there, and I braced on the inside for what I feared might be a very bittersweet meeting. But Gail or perhaps some other force knew what we needed that day. My wife stood and smiled when they came through the door. She took her daughter's face in her hands and pulled her close for a hug and kiss.

Gail, their mother, was there with us the entire hour of the visit, ooing and cooing at her loved ones and other times, just silently smiling. When Darlene gave her a gift, a few new tops in purple and pinks along with some much smaller pants due to her continued weight loss, she smiled and made some beautiful sounds to show how she liked them. Then she proceeded to touch and fold them, a display we took to mean pleasure. The day I had feared that morning turned into a beautifully memorable holiday.

December turned into January, and the rest of the brown leaves fell to the ground covered in frost. People were busy with getting on from the holidays and visits slowed. I felt the contrasted absence of family and found myself as lonely as I could remember. There were plenty of people who came and went—CNAs,

Hospice staff, the occasional kitchen staff who I had become very friendly with, yet there I was, sinking into a long slog of self-pity and loneliness. I've read there is a phenomenon that seems to happen to many during this time of year known as SAD—Seasonal Affective Disorder. Maybe I had a little of this SAD, and maybe the contrast between holiday cheer and the lack of it was adding its own glumness to the long, dark days, but I think all of these were not the basis of what despair lingered around the periphery of my soul. Even prayer, a constant throughout my life, had begun to feel less like talking to God and more like talking into a quiet room. But maybe I had an answer to these prayers, a gift that came in the form of a person, Karen.

I had seen her around and frankly avoided her before then. She was a member of the "gripe club," as I came to call them, in my head of course. They were always complaining about this thing in the dining room, and that thing in the hallway, and another thing altogether at the front desk. Everywhere I went, Karen seemed to be there complaining about something none of us had any control over. Then one day, she confronted me and asked why I always walked away when she was talking. So, I told her the truth. Talking didn't bother me, but more often than not, she and the others weren't conversing; they were venting their negative frustrations, at least that's how it appeared to me. I explained to her that if I participated, that habit would follow me back to the apartment, and it was my responsibility to keep Gail and myself in a positive environment. I don't think Karen appreciated this explanation, at least not in that moment. She turned her wheelchair away from me and zipped away without another word.

After that, I avoided her and the others even more, certain they hadn't gained any warm feelings toward me. Then one day, she wheeled in front of me in the hallway, cutting me off, flustering me so badly that I couldn't think of an excuse to turn around and head the other direction.

"You play Scrabble," she accused, her eyebrows lifting toward the top of her forehead.

"Me? Well... yes, I—"

"I also play Scrabble," she informed me and cocked her head just slightly, while I failed to fill the silence with an invitation.

"From one person who plays Scrabble to the next," she continued, seemingly annoyed, "don't you think it would make sense to play with someone?"

"Don't you have a partner?" I asked, finding my voice and looking around, hoping they'd appear, and I could make my getaway.

"Tomorrow, one o'clock," she said. "I know that's when Gail is usually napping." It wasn't an invitation, and she didn't wait for a rebuttal. "I'll see you then," she concluded and wheeled off, leaving me in a stammering cloud of words I couldn't grab fast enough to decline.

What could I do? It wasn't like me to not make a date. So, the next day at one o'clock, and many days after that, Karen and I played Scrabble. I brought my calm way of playing, and she brought her ever impatient, always flustered, "You're playing too fast, it makes me nervous!" manner. And I loved it. Karen, as it turned out, reminded me so much of my sister, that many times, I slipped and called her Judy, and just as Judy would have, she scolded me for it. I'd never felt so at home at Victory Centre than when Karen fussed about something I couldn't imagine being irritated by. But, like my sister, that was just her way; she didn't mean anything by it. Over time, I appreciated her tendency to share what she felt with openness, and I began to see the good qualities in Karen, too. She had no filter, but she meant what she said, and when she had something positive to say, it held all the more weight.

For a time, we attempted to include more residents in our weekly game, advertising it in the community list of events. But

Karen would inevitably become frustrated with some aspect of each additional participant's play style, personality, or something else completely intangible to me, so we decided to make this our own thing, and that was just fine with both of us.

We would often play in the small lounge area just outside the apartment, or if I needed to keep a closer eye on Gail, I would pop up a small folding table that I'd pulled out of the trash one day after a resident had moved away. Karen would roll up, and we would play until we were interrupted, which was more often than not. Gail would wake up and want to get in on the fun. She'd wander over to the board and grab a few letters, tilt the table, or toss something onto it. Occasionally, she would play with Karen's hair or fiddle with her ear. The first time this happened, I thought it might be the end of our Scrabble sessions. But Karen was always patient in those moments, and I saw a switch flip in her. Karen did have a reserve of calmness and accessed it when needed. There was more to her than I had originally given her credit for.

I wondered whether Gail sensed my closeness to Karen, whether she knew Karen provided something I needed, something that she could not give me. And I wondered whether that made her jealous or if she understood this. I didn't want to give my Gail reason to worry, so I tried to strike a balance between the need for a friend and the need to make sure Gail knew that she would always get the best of me. So when she interrupted our games, I smiled and greeted her but made my best attempt to finish a round before setting the game aside.

One night, after a day when Karen and I had managed a full game of Scrabble, Gail crawled out of bed and startled me with her presence. I was sitting in the living room writing in my journal when she walked up to me and calmly took the pad of paper out of my hand and opened it in front of her face.

"My story," she said.

I nodded. "That's right, Gail. Your story. Our story."

"Kind words are like honey sweet to the soul and healthy for the body." Proverbs 16:24

Chapter Twelve

Stay in the Boat

*I just got back from caregivers group. To me and my situation,
I'm not very enthusiastic about most of the conversation.*

Everything in the apartment sounded like it was tumbling down,
and the only thing louder than the crash and the scream that accompanied it was the fear of a worst-case scenario filling my mind. I
ran to the source of commotion, expecting to find a crumpled heap
of Gail on the floor of our bedroom, everything breakable or heavy
piled high on top of her. My chest was so tight, there was barely
room for air by the time I reached her and found that she was, for
the most part, just fine.

But it was the second fall that week. The first time, she had hit
her head on the lamp and become disoriented, falling to the floor
as though her bones had just disappeared. Somehow, that didn't
leave a mark on her. But this time, she was not so lucky. I don't
know how it happened. When I heard the commotion coming from
the bedroom, I trotted from the kitchen and found her lying in the
closet entrance on her back. I assumed she had been rummaging
through her clothes. She did that often, as though searching for
something to wear, though she was fully clothed in her day's outfit.

I called for a CNA, and we soon had Gail upright and wandering again, something she had begun to do with more frequency as the spring of 2017 marched toward summer. I was overjoyed at first with this new activity, believing it could be the beginning of a halt in decline, maybe even a reversal of her long recent slide. But with the increased activity came these dangers. It was clear there was no improvement in her depth perception or coordination.

I increased my sensitivity to things that could affect her balance, making sure no shoes or other objects were ever left on the floor. I made sure every piece of furniture was firmly against a wall and within reaching distance of the next one, giving her both a free path through the middle of the room and something to grab onto almost anywhere she could stand.

It is scary enough for any old person to sustain an injury; our bodies simply don't heal like they once did, but more so when you are already mobility-impaired. I tried to imagine what Gail struggled with each day and the confusion of what was going on around her. Something as simple as her pajamas not being in the same place they were the previous night could be a frightening experience. A hip break was my greatest concern—a common and awful injury for the elderly and one that would guarantee the loss of Gail's remaining mobility. For now, she had plenty of it. When she was upright, her thin legs were strong. It was her ability to interpret the environment around her that was weak. Adding to my worries, I was told by hospice not to attempt catching Gail if I saw her falling, that I might injure myself and then no longer be able to care for her.

I would continue to tweak the furniture throughout the end of spring and summer, shortening the distance between pieces of furniture or moving small objects to a less-traveled area, like the lamp, a thing that she would often try and fail to use as a stabilizer. After the initial shock of the first falls receded, I was surprisingly at ease with an upturned apartment, and I was becoming better at not trying to make Gail better but rather making things better for her.

Around that time, Darlene tipped me off about a meeting that took place at the Senior Center, which I could see from my apartment window. They were called the Caring Group, a small collection of people from the area who were caregivers to their partners, and whose partners were suffering from similarly compromising afflictions. I was surprised to learn about the group after having lived at Victory Centre for over two and a half years, but I swallowed hurt feelings from not being informed sooner by the staff or members and made plans to attend. I hoped I would find another layer of support and be able to give the same within a community of like-minded and like-afflicted people. What I found there couldn't have been further from that.

"Hi," said a man I knew neither by face nor by name.

I walked to the man and reached out my hand. "Richard," I said. "Nice to meet you."

"Yeah, well... Maybe under different circumstances," he said. "I'm Tom."

I squinted my eyes at Tom, wondering what better circumstances there could be than having support tailored directly to the struggle we all faced.

"I see we have a new visitor to the group," said another voice, and turning, I recognized both the name and face of its owner, though I had only known them since earlier that week when I had come by for information.

"Hi, Renee," I said cheerfully. "Glad to be here."

"Well, why don't we get started," she said, and everyone sat.

Renee had me introduce myself to the group, only a few of whom I knew; the rest I assumed were members of the neighboring community. I don't know what I expected to come next, but I wouldn't have guessed it had you given me one hundred guesses.

"Alright, what are we struggling with lately, gang," said Renee, and everyone laughed, including me.

I made the mistake of thinking she was kidding.

"Nancy has been absolutely exhausting lately," one of the men jumped in. "Nothing I do pleases her. Most of the time, she just sits there and shouts. If she ever remembers me, it's only to say something harsh, that I forgot to empty the dishwasher or her food's gone cold. Well, eat it faster. And empty the damn dishes yourself if you want them done so damned bad."

I waited for Renee to gently remind him that his wife was suffering from a disease she had no control over, that of course this was difficult on him, but what she needed, what they both needed, was every ounce of patience he could muster. And if in her lucid moments she needed him to put up the dishes, there was nothing he could do more loving than that.

"Ha, I hear you," said Renee. "Who else?"

Everyone else.

Each member of the group, to varying degrees, spent the next hour complaining about their partners—their dementia-suffering partners who would love nothing more in the world than to have just one rational thought each day. And it seemed these people wanted nothing more than to be rid of them. This wasn't a support group. This was a justification group, a place for these "caregivers" to feel better about their desire to move on with their lives.

I couldn't understand it. Not the wanting to be free from the burden; of course I could understand that. Any feeling human would want their last years to be a splendid ride off into the sunset like we see in many movies, to be two people, healthy minds and bodies well into their nineties, until they peacefully die in each other's arms one starry and blissful night. But wouldn't a feeling human also want what's best for that person they have that fantasy with, no matter what the reality?

As I sat there, all I could think was how, at that very moment, their loved ones were in beds or chairs alone somewhere…in pain, confused, scared, craving in whatever way they could for the comfort of connection. And here were the people charged with giving them that connection, who should want to give it to them. Here they were, complaining about how hard their own lives are when they haven't the slightest idea how hard it is behind the shroud of cognitive loss. Then I thought about my own darling love, alone in our apartment as I grew increasingly frustrated in my chair. I couldn't stand it anymore.

"You're wrong," I said, standing up as suddenly my old legs could. "Every one of you. This isn't a support group. You should be with your loved ones, supporting them and each other in doing that…not doing whatever this is!"

And with that, I left and walked with steady steps across the parking lot and back to my apartment. And when I was inside, I walked to Gail and took her in my arms and held her. "Thank you," I said. "I love you. Just the way you are and every other way you'll ever be. I want you to know that."

"Husband," she managed, and she squeezed me back.

That night, after Gail was asleep, I lay in my bed fuming about what I had seen and heard at the Caring Group. It took some time and a quiet apartment to realize why. I saw myself in every one of them. Each complainer had, in their own words, voiced a frustration I had also felt. I prided myself on tamping those feelings down so quickly that they never affected Gail, but had I truly? Had there never been a moment when I allowed my frustrations to slip past my eyes or off my tongue?

My gut sank, and I wished I had my exit from the Caring Group to do over again. I didn't agree with the caustic venting. I couldn't see what that could possibly help. But I could have empathized with the reasons. Caregiving is hard, harder than you ever imagine it to be before it is thrust upon you. I could have allowed that much for them. For me. After all, we hadn't left our loved ones. Whatever our failures, that wasn't one of them.

That night in my journal, after I had written about my experience with the Caring Group, I concluded with, "We're going through the storm, and there is often only room for two of us. But we are in this boat together, and this boat is holding up just fine."

"Rejoice always, pray without ceasing, give thanks in all circumstances; for this is the will of God in Christ Jesus for you." 1 Thessalonians 5:16-18

Chapter Thirteen
Less is More

Whew – some quiet alone moments. Not meant as a complaint.
The privilege far outweighs any discomfort.

"Hi Gail! Hello? Is she there, Richard?"

I turned the volume up. "We're here, Isabelle. We're just trying to catch up. Gail, do you know who that is? Do you know who Isabelle is?"

Gail was sitting in her chair, rocking ever so slightly as she had been for the last twenty or so minutes, staring intently toward something only she could see.

"Gail, your mother is turning one hundred today. Did you know today was your mother's birthday?"

Gail made a sound like something between a glottal stop and a hoarse hum.

"She's so happy you called, Isabelle. Having trouble speaking up right now, but she knows. She knows…"

She didn't know. She hadn't known the significance of any date for several months now—not Valentine's Day, not our 61st wedding anniversary in March, and not birthdays, neither her mother's 100th nor her own 80th. Gail lived in the everyday, minute-by-minute existence afforded by her condition, and I lived there with her. Numbers on a calendar no longer meant anything. She didn't even seem to know what a calendar was.

She could see my journal, however, and had become increasingly fixated on it, even antagonistic.

If she ever caught me writing, this surge of energy seemed to come from somewhere deep within, enough to propel her toward me and pull at the cover or pages. More than once, she tore a few out. "No, Gail," I would say, pulling the book away. She wouldn't argue, but an almost petulant silence always followed. Sometimes, if I forgot to put the journal away after making my entry, I would find it scribbled in. Those sections, I marked "Gail was here."

She seemed to know it was about her and yet seemed almost jealous of it. Between that and Scrabble, I'm not sure which she was most bothered by. When I went out for the increasingly rare nine holes of golf, she didn't seem to fluster, not when I put on my clothes or strapped on my shoes or hauled the clubs through the apartment. "Have a nice round, honey," she seemed to say with her silence.

But pick up the journal… Even if she was in another room, she would come trotting in. I had to start hiding the thing from her after separate incidents of returning to find pages crumpled on the floor or missing altogether. Soon, around that time, I would be away less and less often, so it wouldn't matter.

I was driving to the grocery store when I found myself unable to rotate my head far enough left or right to properly check my blind spots. I'd been having neck stiffness for years, likely a complication from my ankylosing spondylitis, a life-long spine condition. Now I had reached a point, and more likely passed it, where it had become dangerous. There had been a few times, I'm ashamed to admit, when I had come to a left turn and, having to rely on all the information I could collect from peripheral vision only, just floored it. I called Darlene.

"You mean we don't have to have 'the talk'?" she said.

"The talk?"

"The talk, Dad. The one every child dreads and never goes well. The talk! Taking your keys away!"

"Oh. Hah! I suppose not."

I decided to take my keys away from myself, which put a damper on golf, a final blow really. With Gail's new normal, my favorite outdoor activity had already slowed to once a month if I was lucky. I was sad when I realized this would likely be the end of my love affair with the little white ball, but Gail was worth any sacrifice. I would need to work around the bus schedule to make the necessary jaunt to the store or bank, another damper on my independence, but when compared with what Gail was going through, I had little reason to complain. It even brought more appreciation for all the years Gail managed without a driver's license. She had done it, so could I.

One benefit of tossing away the keys was the increased relationship with Stephen, my grandson. He lived only five minutes away and volunteered regularly to take me grocery shopping in lieu of the bus or a cab. After a few weeks of this, I learned that he, too, had an affinity for Scrabble. Soon we were locked in competitive seven-letter tilts, with Stephen, as he would put it, making sure I didn't cheat. I never cheated; I just took advantage of "all" the rules. As time went on, Stephen and I became close. He was more than a grandson to me; he was a friend and someone I trusted. A cooking enthusiast, he often made meals for Gail and me or dropped off freshly baked cookies. He became a relief valve for Darlene and Bill when they were away. Had I known the great relationship I would gain in my grandson, I might have given up the car years before.

Even if I had not suffered from visibility-reducing neck stiffness, being at the apartment was becoming increasingly necessary. Even though most of the time, Gail would appear feeble and generally incapable of mischief, she would sometimes surprise me. I would return after being gone only a few minutes to grab breakfast or visit a neighboring resident and find her rocking chair across the room or the mattress dragged onto the floor. If she could do that, then she could pull those things on top of herself. She couldn't if I was there.

The scariest part of the new normal was called hyper-orality. I was in the kitchen when I heard a muffled, clicking, gurgling sound. I ran into the living room and found a wide-eyed Gail looking back at me with what I can only describe as the guilty eyes of a child caught. There was another "click." It was coming from her mouth.

"What's in your mouth, Gail?"

Click…gurgle.

"Spit it out, Gail."

Click, gurgle, click…her eyes still locked on mine. Then she made a slight gagging motion, and I panicked.

I ran to her and squeezed her cheeks, breaking the seal of her lips. That only revealed tightly clenched teeth determined to hold the hidden prize.

"Do not swallow it, Gail!" I shouted as I ran out of our apartment toward the front desk, screaming, "Code nine! Code nine!" the signal for a medical emergency, then jogged back up the stairs with the CNA taking two steps at a time. It's amazing how fear seemed to take twenty years off my limbs.

We flew through the door to Gail, whose eyes were wide as saucers. It was like the older sibling had tattled, and now a parent had shown up. But still, she would not willingly give up her treasure. Either Gail realized the futility of the situation, or the CNA applied more strength than I could muster. It only took a few seconds to pry Gail's mouth open and reveal a plastic cap from a water bottle. I found the bottle half full in the fridge, no spill. How she managed this, I will never know.

I spent the rest of that day searching for and purging or hiding all items that could fit in Gail's mouth. Apparently, as Darlene would inform me from her research after I related the event, hyper-orality was common in the later stages of cognitive decline. *Later stages...* As always, I didn't focus on the implications of that reality but on how I could mitigate the complications. How much time we had left, I would leave in God's hands. How well we could spend that time, that was my responsibility.

"But the one who endures to the end will be saved."
Matthew 24:13

Chapter Fourteen

A Shared Language

Then we went outside with the wheelchair.
We're back and Gail ate a whole dish of ice cream
with whip cream and chocolate syrup.

Even when they had become scarce, I don't think I realized just how important coherent moments from Gail were, until they weren't there anymore.

I could usually count on one or two responses from Gail in the form of "yes" or "no," a nod or a headshake each day. There would be the random statement of fact or an exclamation about something she did or didn't like, usually about me or food or cleanliness. It was around the same time that Gail first started putting problematic things into her mouth that nearly every lucid word stopped coming out of it.

She would still smile and acknowledge visitors in the apartment or as we passed by a person with Gail in her wheelchair. She would utter an occasional "sure" or a prolonged "ohhh…" But these seemed to come more sparingly and rarely in response to being communicated with.

"Good morning, Gail. Are you ready to get cleaned up?"
Mumbles.

"Gail, are you hungry? We need to get you cleaned up before you eat."

Finger fidgeting along with mumbles.

"How 'bout a song, Gail? Would you like to hear a song?"

Squirming, finger wringing, then picking at something invisible in the carpet.

And so our day went.

One silent morning, she started to hold mouthfuls of breakfast for long periods after chewing before eventually swallowing, leading to a nearly two-hour feeding routine. Afterward, while she tried to pick the painted border of colorful fruits from the rim of the plate, I set about cleaning up the food that had found its way to the floor. I removed Gail's bib and tossed it in the sink for later, then cleaned the table and waited for Gail to inspect it. This had become a daily ritual I'd come to enjoy more than coffee. After I wiped the table free of food, she would swipe her arm over it like a windshield wiper, and if she found any remaining bits of food in the cracks, she would tap at them until I finished the job. It was one of the few ways she consistently communicated with me, a little thing I held onto. I looked forward to it every morning.

After breakfast, I thought it might be a good idea to break up the scenery with a wheelchair stroll around the grounds.

"I'd like a walk, Gail. Do you want to go on a stroll with me?"

She babbled in a way that sounded like a baby humming while mouthing a pacifier. It sounded nothing like a "yes" or "no," but there was something in it that I understood to mean agreement. I often remarked to Darlene that if they could translate the hieroglyphics of ancient Egypt, I couldn't understand why no one had yet translated the sounds of people like Gail. There were many times when I felt like I understood it clearly, though I could never have explained how or specifically what words were being used, only that I "felt" the meaning.

I set up Gail in her wheelchair and pushed us out the doorway into the hall. It was a bright, late morning. I commented on the wonderful light coming through the window at the end of the hall.

"Would you like to go see it, Gail?"

She babbled, and again, I was certain of the answer. The realization that we were communicating filled me with energy like no amount of caffeine could. So, I continued chatting with my wife, and she continued babbling to me in sounds that I was becoming increasingly aware of the meaning of. I kept my side of the conversation to simple yes-or-no questions, and she responded with what I took to be yes-or-no sounds.

As we approached the doorway, she called out a series of excited mumbles without any prompting from myself, and to my surprise, without really thinking about it, I responded, but not with words... at least, not words that would be intelligible to anyone else. I let out a series of sounds similar to Gail's but responding to the tone and feeling carried within them. It felt like mimicking the way an animal sounds or another language. And then, she spoke to me in this language, and I realized I did know what she was communicating, not fluently, but just enough to get by.

We carried on like this, her offering wordless opinions on our walk and me doing my best to respond with my modified echoes. We were together not just in physical form but in communication. She was more with me than I had felt in some time. I pushed us down the canopy-covered front walkway lined with benches and nodded to a few sitting residents, then down the paved path to the gazebo where Gail and I liked to sit and watch butterflies or pet dogs on leashes. All the while, we continued in our language of sounds.

As we approached the gazebo, we passed a fellow resident whose eyes showed he had heard the back-and-forth. An apologetic shrug was all I could offer in explanation. To my surprise, another resident wandered by, a small woman perhaps ten years our senior. She had come around the corner during one of our exchanges, and the look on her face reflected that she clearly understood, not the sounds we were making, but their purpose. I couldn't help wondering if she was a caregiver to a loved one like Gail. This prompted a frightening thought that Gail's recent decline might not be her slipping further from me, but rather, me slipping closer to her. Had she stopped communicating with the English language because she sensed somehow that I no longer needed it? After a moment's pondering, I shrugged my shoulders. What did it matter whether one reality was more true, or both?

After a long walk that took us down the main hallways and along the perimeter walk around Victory Centre, I directed us back inside and toward the cafeteria to see what was on the menu. I wasn't planning to keep us there, not with Gail in my charge. I don't know if this was a change in me or in the environment around me, but it seemed increasingly toxic in the shared spaces. Most conversations contained gossip, complaining, or bullying, like we had all stopped maturing and had begun regressing back into grade school.

I hated it. I had come to a place where I no longer felt the strength to confront it. That was hard for me, a lifelong member of the ministry meant to lead or point people in the direction of a better life. I don't know how often I succeeded in that, but I tried. Gail was my new mission on earth, and I could no longer serve two purposes. I needed to keep my focus where it belonged, so I gathered our food and wheeled us back to the apartment where we ate lunch much more efficiently than breakfast. Afterward, I sat with her in the living room, and she soon fell into a nap.

I took the opportunity to play against my alter ego, Dick, in Scrabble. I was only a few words in, losing to Dick, when Gail's Scrabble senses woke her, and she reminded me that even when asleep, I was supposed to be paying attention to her. Every word I played, she showed me how she would prefer the letters to be arranged. Who was I to argue? Perhaps she was trying to teach me words in this new language we were sharing. I placed the word "GRAPES," pulling in front of Dick by a few points, and Gail changed it to "GAR SE P."

"Gar-se-pe," I mouthed, and Gail muttered something similar back.

"I suppose it's you and me playing now, Gail," I smiled.

Mumbled affirmation.

I apologized to Dick that I would not be able to finish, and Gail and I played our modified Scrabble game until she realized she had my full attention and went back to napping.

I smiled watching her for a while. I couldn't think of anything I would rather be doing with these precious remaining years than exactly what I was doing. I chanced grabbing my journal for a few entries. I liked to sit at the small table overlooking the parking lot and front entrance. It made me feel like I was with Gail, writing out our shared reality while staying connected to the one everyone else saw. This lasted only a few minutes. Like a button was pushed, Gail was soon up, fidgeting with the pages.

"Now, how am I supposed to write your story if you won't let me, huh?" I scrunched my eyes over a wry smile.

She replied with equally wry mumbling.

"You can play with the journal, Gail, so long as you remember that I'm the boss here," I said, knowing that we both knew that wasn't true.

She paused for a moment, gave me a mischievous look, then pulled her hands into fists and put both in front of her, like she was ready to box me using the Marquess of Queensbury rules. Then she dropped them, smiled, and laughed, and in clear words I thought were lost to us, she said, "I'm the boss." It was the brightest her eyes had been in weeks, all Gail with no cloud of dementia to be seen.

"Ok!" I said, gleefully. "You win! I give. I know better than to tangle with you, Gail." I tried to manage a smile, but something new ached in me. It might have been the first time, after a long stretch of decline, that I wasn't entirely excited for the cloud to pass. The sun still warmed my face, but I felt no real hope in it. This hurt like nothing else. It was the first time I allowed myself to accept that Gail would never be "better," that this passing of the clouds was only that, and there would be darker storms on the horizon. However, I reached out and touched my Gail lovingly. We would face the darkness together.

Later that month, a checkup with her doctor deemed Gail to be past the "moderate" stage in her progression into dementia. It was time to make some difficult decisions about the future.

"He stilled the storm to a whisper; the waves of the sea were hushed." Psalm 107:29

Chapter Fifteen

Mightier than the Sword

*I'm learning the only way we can navigate dementia together is
for me to get in the boat, and together we will learn how to move
through the deepening water. I will follow her lead.*

A moment came not long after Gail and I developed our new
language together and my realization that this voyage we were
on was the last one we had left, a moment that solidified all of
this in my mind, if not yet my heart. To the doctor, it seemed like
a casual event, one like the twenty or so others he'd had that day.
To me, it was a eulogy for our former life, an elegy to our current
one when he uttered…

"We need to discuss CPR and feeding tubes."

I'm sure I looked at him stunned for a few moments before
parroting his words dumbly back.

"It's just a formality, but…it is important, Richard. She's past
moderate, so we just need to decide what happens if she needs
them."

"Needs them?"

"To be resuscitated. Or put on life support—feeding tubes,
breathing apparatus—that sort of thing."

I didn't answer. I couldn't. I knew with certainty what Gail would have wanted. "If God's ready for me, I'm ready for Him," she would have said. She had said as much on the few occasions during our life when such morbid conversations would pop up. But I knew with equal certainty that I could not make that decision for her. For us. I knew it had to be made, but it simply wasn't in me to make it.

Like all other things of this nature, Darlene was the one who, with the power of attorney we had given her, made the decision. I let her do that without me present, and she signed the proper papers according to what Gail would have wanted. It wasn't long before that when Darlene accompanied me to the funeral home in Bartlett, and we sat there for what seemed a very long time. We did up both our wills, including decisions on burial versus cremation, whether there would be a viewing and service at the funeral home, and what would be done with our ashes. I could not have gotten through that period without my daughter.

When we were back at the apartment from the doctor's appointment, I found I had received a letter from my pen pal, Dr. Helen Brown. Helen is the president of a company that provides education to facilities and staff on how to support those living with dementia. She had spent significant time studying how to thwart some of the common symptoms of dementia, focusing on the social, emotional, physical, and spiritual well-being of memory care patients. She must have heard of my daily journaling from someone at Victory Centre and decided to reach out, saying she was interested in seeing some entries. She said it could be a help to their mission. I sent a portion of the journal, expecting a polite "never mind."

After a few days, I received a letter, surprising me with compliments—my scrawling contained not only raw and honest feelings any caregiver could relate to but also helpful thoughts and concepts around the act of caregiving itself. I wrote back, thanking her, and to my surprise, she responded again, asking if we could meet in person. I accepted and was immediately impressed by her truly empathetic and caring nature. We had been monthly pen pals ever since.

In the newest letter I received, Helen asked what I had meant in a previous correspondence when I mentioned the phrase "get in the boat." I had scribbled it thoughtlessly, something I told myself from time to time as a reminder that Gail and I were in this thing together but that neither of us really were captains and couldn't control the weather or the seas. My job was simply to do my best to keep us afloat and protect Gail, my precious cargo.

Helen wanted a more complete picture of what being with a person with dementia is like from my perspective and how I saw my role as a caregiver to her. I did my best to explain, but so much of my understanding of this position was wound up in my feelings about the situation, the instincts that kept me charting in the right direction. Being "in the boat" is a personal journey, but at the same time, it gave me a sense of fulfillment just knowing that I was exactly where I needed to be, doing exactly what I was supposed to be doing. For me, all it really meant was realizing I could not pull the boat along or push it forward from behind. I just had to be willing to step inside, take a seat, and accept the journey both of us were on, guiding us away from rocks and shoals the best I could.

I didn't know it yet, but Helen had designs for "get in the boat" that were much greater than simply understanding it academically. Soon after the letter, she called me.

"Richard." She said my name in that tone people use to ask you whether you are up for a conversation deeper than a puddle.

"Yes?"

"I have a proposal for you."

"Well, you're a swell gal, Helen, but you know I'm happily married." I chuckled, and it disappeared into an awkward silence.

"That's just what I want to talk about, Richard," she said with no hint of humor returned. "Most husbands looking after wives like Gail aren't happily married."

I began to worry about where this conversation was headed.

"Look, I read through your letter about 'get in the boat,' and...I think you might have something worth sharing here."

Helen explained that she had shared my thoughts with others in her circle and administrators at various memory care and elderly care facilities. All were interested in hearing more. She called it a summit, an event where people in the memory care, assisted living, and supportive living community would meet and discuss ideas related to making life better for sufferers and their caregivers. She wanted me to come. She also wanted me to give a talk about the concept of "get in the boat."

"A talk? Me?"

"Who else?"

I could think of about seven billion someone else's, but when Helen was set on something, there was little one could do to sway her. I agreed to think about it, silently planning to give it the respectful minimum amount of time before politely declining.

Over the next few hours, I imagined what such a "talk" might be like. It was a simple concept—you just got in the boat and stopped trying to control everything. *Everything.* I pictured all the little things dementia did through Gail daily. *People won't really understand unless they are here in the apartment with us*, I reasoned. After all, this wasn't the kind of thing you could simply explain in a few minutes on stage. Even those with the best imagination wouldn't feel enough. They wouldn't ache and boil and laugh uncontrollably, all things one needed to feel and do to really understand. They had to see it.

They had to see it!

I called Helen back the same day, after reasoning my way into a commitment to the very thing I was supposed to be avoiding. I pitched the idea.

"A skit!" I said.

"A skit? I don't think there's ever been a skit at the Summit," she said more like a thought to herself than a response to me.

I felt myself flush with nerves. Suddenly, I feared losing this opportunity, a stark contrast to my feelings earlier, and I almost laughed when I said, "It's the only way, Helen! No one will understand unless they see it. Your colleagues, even you, you just don't know—"

"Ok! It's brilliant, Richard!"

"It is?"

"It has to be a skit! I'm convinced!" she said. Then after a moment's pause, "…We just need an actor to play Gail."

"Well, Helen, you see, we already have our actor. I'm talking to her now," I stammered.

"…I don't know, Richard…"

It took convincing to get Helen to agree to sit in for Gail on stage and perform in front of an audience. But ultimately, she saw what to me was obvious. Outside of myself and family, she was the one who knew the most about the life Gail and I shared. She also had the best working knowledge of the sporadic and often unpredictable behavior dementia sufferers exhibited. She could mimic everything Gail did—throw a fit, hold a mumbled conversation with imaginary friends or myself—it was exactly what the audience needed to see. And the beauty of the "get in the boat" concept was that no matter what Helen did, my job didn't change. I simply accepted it and did my best to make her comfortable. That was the clarity of purpose which made these the best years of Gail's and my marriage, the same one that needed to be on stage.

Helen said there would need to be an introduction to who Gail and I were, our life at Victory Centre, and our relationship to herself. So, we held a few impromptu rehearsals, one every couple of weeks. Each meeting was different, owing to Gail's attendance and her reaction to all that she saw. And each time, we learned that we needed some other element to round out the "performance." In the end, I felt like I had the easy job, something like a curator of an art exhibit. My job was not to make Helen, playing Gail, behave in any particular way but simply to display her to the world.

By the time of the summit, any nerves I might have felt during the process were dissolved by Helen's and her incredible team of volunteers' understanding and kindness. Helen's performance was wonderful. She stepped into the boat we had made for the skit. She babbled. She laughed. We even danced. I gave something of a speech, nothing more than simple words from my experience. As I spoke, Helen nodded and smiled as Gail might have.

When we were done, I saw more than one pair of glistening eyes in the crowd as they stood and clapped. I guided "Gail" to stand and held her hand high in the air. She and I stepped out of the makeshift wooden vessel...and I returned to the real boat, the true inspiration for it all, my work of art, my love.

"Husbands, love your wives and do not be harsh with them."
Colossians 3:19

Chapter Sixteen

Wings over the Water

*Sitting across from Gail as she smiles is a breathtaking
time for me, a privilege; I cannot explain it.*

I don't know whether Gail was more present with me in the weeks
following my performance of *Get in the Boat*, or whether that feeling was fabricated by my excitement at having done something
of such significance for my wife. It had always been her and me
in the boat together, but somehow, after sharing that concept with
so many, it felt like we were both rowing now. She hadn't been on
stage with me, but I believed she knew. That feeling stayed with
me long after November of 2018 when I shared our lives together.
Before winter turned to spring, it would be clear once again that I
was the only one holding an oar.

Fingering through family picture books was a constant for
Gail and me, both a prescribed activity to engage her self-identity
and sense of belonging to others, and a low-risk use of her time
that we could do together. The decline in recognition had come in
plateaus and descents. When we first arrived at Victory Centre, she
still seemed to know most of the faces in those sleeves. Soon after,
dementia took away her most distant relations, second cousins,
and friends from long ago. Eventually, the same happened with

nearer family, grandchildren, cousins, and siblings. Like ripples in the water with Gail at the center, each faded until there were only those nearest.

When Darlene or I were on the page, sometimes she would squint hard, fighting against her macular degeneration to put thought to a recognition she felt. She would squint hard with her right eye, the only one with vision left, trying to bring memory into focus. Sometimes, she would place a hand on the book, as if saying she didn't want to turn another page. Consistently, she wished to stay with those photos longer.

I was still there, along with her and her children. Sometimes, she would pull these photos from their sleeves and flip them forward and back, almost as if playing peekaboo. There was still a connection, a fondness, a light that shone in the dim recesses of remembrance when I pointed at those pictures…

Until there wasn't.

The last ripples fanned outward, then faded away. I had always known it would. It hurt, but it was not a surprise. Then February of 2019 came. As we sat looking at a family album Darlene had made of one of our Christmases together, Gail did surprise me. There were no more memories to fade, or so I thought, but I had forgotten the last piece. I pointed to a picture of Gail and there was no change in her countenance. Her eyes had no light of recognition. It was as if the woman sitting beside me had ceased to exist.

Photos had been the last place Gail seemed to exist to herself, visually. There was a moment after a haircut, more than a year before. The beautician had cut her hair shorter than usual, and Gail's curls were gone. She stood facing the mirror, pulling at her hair and quietly murmuring in a sad and hollow voice. Gail had always loved wearing her hair in curls, a rare thing when so many don't embrace their natural beauty. I had originally assumed she was just disappointed that the shape of her hair was so changed.

But after that, whenever she looked at herself in the mirror, it was as if she only saw a stranger there.

As she stared at the photo of herself laying in her lap, I wondered whether she saw herself in that piece of paper. Did she know herself at all?

The next morning, I woke to the sound of a loud alarm, and some instinct from my past had me reaching for a clock by my bedside that didn't exist. I hadn't needed to set a morning alarm in decades. I sat up and focused through the grogginess until I realized that this was no alarm in our room but a siren.

I looked over at Gail sleeping soundly through the clamor. Her hands, once so full of life, lay softly at rest, each wrinkle telling a story of all the years dedicated to her family. When she was asleep, it seemed like she was away in another world, one I hoped kept her out of the grasp of dementia. I often prayed she was dreaming visions of vibrant youth or surrounded by our happy children, unencumbered with the weight of illness.

I slowly rolled away from this peaceful vision and after a slow arching of my back to stretch some of the pain out of my lower spine, I ambled over to my morning perch. Outside the window, where I would wave to the nurses and other staff members arriving for the day, there was an ambulance slowing to a stop.

I can't say I ever grew used to seeing the ambulances arrive a few times each week. Living in a senior living facility, it was a part of life, and I knew one day they would come for me or Gail. That day, there were four arrivals. The next day, there were seven.

It was the worst flu outbreak I'd seen since Gail and I moved to Victory Centre, the worst I'd seen period. It seemed like every hour paramedics were carting away neighbors down our hall. We had all been vaccinated, that was mandatory. But influenza is an ever-changing virus, one that vaccines can only hope to follow closely behind as it charts its way through adaptation.

The next day, I awoke to the first effects of what was already in my system. Nausea, fever, chills, fatigue, loss of appetite, and pain. My instinct was to quarantine myself from Gail, to protect her from this dangerous invader. I called the nurses' station and asked about exactly how to do that. The response was simple and obvious. I couldn't. If I was infected, then it had already been in my system for days. Gail either had it already and symptoms would surface soon, or her immune system had fought it off and no good could be gained by separating us.

There was, however, a great deal of bad if either of us encountered others who weren't yet exposed. Gail and I would have to be quarantined after all, together in our own apartment.

The flu is a mortal threat to the elderly. Our immune systems are weaker, our metabolism of life-sustaining nutrition and medicine slower. What causes most of the population to simply call into work or skip a few days of school very often causes an aged person to make sure their estate is in order and to call their family and friends to tell them just how much they are loved.

The quarantine was a lonely time. Even though I had Gail with me, and thankfully she was not sick, it was moments like these my wife's absence was more keenly felt. Earlier in our life, illness meant she would have been making me soup and monitoring my temperature, changing out cool moist rags on my forehead, and holding my hand. But Gail could not do those things anymore. Even though my body was drained by a feverish heat, and I trembled violently from the cold aching every hour of the day, it was still Gail that needed my care more than I needed hers. I had the flu, and that would last a week if I was fortunate, but she had something that was never over, never got better, and would never be fortunate.

My care of Gail during the flu episode was no more than minimal; I had no more than that to offer. Most days, between meals and cleanings, and my constant trips to the bathroom where illness ravaged my intestines, I would place her fidget blanket in her lap and hope the snaps, buttons, and various gadgets attached to it would be enough to hold her attention, at least giving me some space to attend to my own needs and rest. And most of the time, it worked. The flu exacerbated the stiffness in my neck, turning into intense pain, and it was difficult for me to even sit, much less stand and follow Gail around. One afternoon, she walked into the bedroom, and I listened from the bed for the telltale sounds of mischief. I heard nothing and assumed she was fussing with her bed linens. After a few moments of silence, I slowly opened my eyes and found my wife walking toward me with my neck pillow. She handed it to me, and so I placed it behind my neck and thanked her, telling her how helpful it was. How was it that she was still looking after me when all else of her seemed gone? I closed my eyes and thanked God for the time we still had together.

During that time of illness, as I gained my strength back and the fever dissipated, leaving my mind a little clearer, I thought about how most people living in senior communities rarely received visitors. That was the life of the marginalized—out of sight, out of mind. "Maybe next month," their family would say to them, but next month might never come. I felt a great competition of feelings—the intense gratitude that my family was so present and supportive of me and Gail throughout these trying years…but also guilt that I was no more deserving than the other wonderful people who sat alone day after day, week after week, until their number was finally called.

After a week of a slow climb upward into recovery, I was cleared for contact with the outside world. I was so grateful the flu had decided to leave Gail alone. And now, it was time to get back to caring for her. We were running low on a few essentials, so I decided I would take the bus to Target.

As I checked the bus schedule and prepped my list, I noticed Gail sitting in her chair, quietly pulling at strings on her doll and rocking slightly. It had been some time since her TTT had faded to a manageable level, only appearing in occasional short bursts here and there. I thought about our usual treks wheeling around Victory Centre, me using the handles of her wheelchair as a rolling walker, her smiling at the passing scenery. "The buses are wheelchair compatible…" I mused, wondering if it was not only me who needed an excursion. A few minutes later, I had cleared the event with staff, and we were sitting together on a bench under the green awning of the entrance waiting for our bus.

I had to accept the adept help of the Victory Centre bus driver loading and unloading Gail and her wheelchair onto the bus. Otherwise, we were autonomous, and the trip was a complete success, taking a little over two hours. Gail smiled practically the whole time, pointing and making sounds at signs, buildings, and the various items on the shelves at Target. We rolled down nearly every aisle. I would push the chair close to a colorful shirt, and she would touch the cloth and smile. She lit up most when I found a pot of African Violets, her favorite flower. They had grown like weeds everywhere we lived except Victory Centre. I pulled the pot from the shelf and placed it in her hands, and Gail clutched it like a treasured possession. It was the most engaged I had seen her in many months and filled me with all the energy in the world, despite having just endured much of the previous week kneeling beside the toilet.

That evening at our little dining table, I sat quietly resting my eyes on Gail. Her focus flitted from one object to the next, seeming more attentive to the world around her. I didn't know if she was aware of my presence, but I was aware of hers. It was her and me, together in the boat.

A flutter sounded outside, and both of our attentions were drawn to the little window beside us. Soft shadows fell on the pane, and soon after, two doves landed softly on the windowsill, a mated pair. When we were younger, Gail would always remark on how doves mated for life. Anytime she saw them, she couldn't help herself; she always reminded me.

Sitting at the table, Gail pointed to the doves and made a cooing sound. She reached her hand out and gently touched the window. It was winter, and the pane was cold. She pulled her hand back but kept looking at the doves, smiling. And then she cooed and giggled. I smiled and added my coos to the chorus between her and the pair of doves. She turned and smiled at me, cooing. My Gail, my gentle dove, my mate for life...

"Do not deliver the soul of Your turtledove to the wild beast; Do not forget the life of Your afflicted forever." Psalm 74:19

Chapter Seventeen
Together, Always

Jim, a dementia patient here, passed away four months after hospice discharged him. He was doing good, denied the benefits of hospice and within a short time his quality of life and health suffered resulting in his death.

Gail's uptick in attentiveness and activity seemed sustained in the days and weeks following our quarantine. Even TTT increased enough to present a great challenge for me, once again. My own constitution was not what it had been even a couple years before. It was not lost on me, the nurses, or my family that my similarly aged, dementia-suffering wife seemed to have more stamina and even more mobility than I did at times.

Neither I nor all the experts in the field seemed to know what caused these rebounds. I liked to believe it was just her, that somewhere in there, Gail was fighting to stay connected. I was proud of her, my fierce Gail. Like so many years previously, she did all she could to remain by my side through the adventures of life. But as with every new normal in this journey, any positive came with an opposite, and sometimes more than equal, negative.

"One could say…she's not dying fast enough," I remarked to a CNA one afternoon, the dried trail of tears still on my face. The

CNA was not our first visitor that day. Before her, we had a routine visit from a member of the hospice team assigned to Gail's care, a visit in which we were informed that they could no longer document any signs of Gail's condition worsening, and she no longer qualified for hospice care.

As hard as it had been for me to accept hospice care for Gail in the first place, it was even harder for it to go. This meant more work for me—no more social workers, dietitians, nursing visits, clergy, and other hospice support workers to share the load of watching and caring for Gail. The ones who knew us most would still stop in and check on my wife and me when they were making their rounds with other patients, but they were busy, and Gail was no longer in their charge. This meant we were back to me and the understaffed CNAs shouldering the load, and my shoulders were not so strong as they had once been. But the most difficult part of losing hospice care was not the physical toll but the one inside— hope.

There can be so much pain in hoping. You know the truth with all your logical thinking faculties, that you are not going to become the first person in history to witness their loved one recover from dementia. You know this as certainly as the sun rises, as certain as the doctors who make it their single most important job to remind you each time you meet with them. This knowledge lives in you every minute of every day while you care for that person who is slowly slipping away. And yet, alongside this knowledge lives a hope, that somehow your loved one will be the exception. A time of seemingly apparent recovery happens and suddenly, that spark of hope is fanned into a flame. Maybe they could hang on just long enough for some new drug to come to market, one that could halt or even reverse the condition. But you know the truth. This time is like the last time. She is not coming back. You douse the flame to keep it from burning down the boat, and you keep paddling.

There were occasional moments of great joy during those difficult months. Gail's memory broke through once, remembering a former Victory Centre CNA she liked very much. Her name was Carrie, and she had helped take care of Gail for years before leaving us. She came to visit Gail one day, unexpectedly, and Gail remembered her as Cherry. We laughed and Gail smiled and murmured and hugged Carrie.

There were some times when Gail seemed to smile at me when she mumbled something, and I could almost see recognition in her eyes. For just a minute or two, I was her husband again, and she was my wife. A flicker. Once when Darlene came for a visit, Gail looked at Darlene, really looked at her and said, "daughter" and smiled. She stayed engaged with Darlene, touching her daughter's arms and even combing her fingers through her hair, like Darlene was her child again. It had been more than a year since Gail had recognized any of her family. More flickers. Were they real or hoped for? Were these the signs of a wife and mother still sometimes present with her loved ones? Were they the tender affections of the shadow of a person no longer there, like echoes left behind?

Feelings twist between joy and grief in these moments. A spark threatens to go up in flames and needs to be put out. Hope, that place that had always been a refuge for me, needed to be kept where it was most useful to us. Gail was not coming back. This lack of deterioration hospice had noted would eventually give way, and she would descend again. Would it stop? No. It may pause for a time. But it would never stop. I knew this to be true. The younger Richard may have held onto hope when hospice left us, using his rooted positivity to entertain the idea that if hospice wasn't needed, maybe that was a sign of good. I could not allow myself to hope like that anymore. It did no good for me…or Gail. But there was something I could still hope for—her comfort…prolonged resilience…and more happy moments with myself and our family. I could hold onto this hope while dashing the other.

During one of Darlene's visits, she questioned openly what we all had wondered at some point. "What if it is all clear to her? What if she does understand what's going on, and every word we say? Should we not talk about her, in front of her? What if we are missing out on being present with her, I mean really being with her, by not sharing these moments of all that is happening?"

I felt anger toward my daughter for saying these things, and I hated myself for it as well. The same thoughts had always lingered in my mind, that Gail was a prisoner trapped behind a viewing glass, seeing and hearing all but never able to participate. But hearing Darlene speak these thoughts into the air made it more real, and that hurt even more. How could I live with myself knowing I had been engaging with my wife as a shell of a person, treating her like a child—correcting behavior, spoon-feeding, talking in babbles and mumbles—and she was powerless, just watching it all unfold? And how could you know this? In so many ways, it was more comfortable to believe Gail wasn't aware, that she didn't have to endure that pain and frustration, and that I wasn't causing it.

"Who can say?" I said with a smile, swallowing the pain. "Who can say...?"

During Gail's worst times, I struggled with being away from her. She might fall while I wasn't there, or there might be a breakthrough I would miss. Being away meant missing out on what could be the last real moments with my wife. It was always a CNA or Darlene who would remind me I wasn't doing Gail or myself, or anybody else any good by isolating. It was causing my health to deteriorate. Not only was I avoiding outside human contact, which was like sustenance to my social personality, but I was no longer walking and had scarcely felt the outside air. Without hospice, I had very little opportunity to be away, and I wanted to be around Gail, waiting for the next moment.

At the urging of Darlene, I decided to attend a block party for residents held in the Victory Centre parking lot right outside our window. It was a chance for everyone to get together during a time of year when the risk of contagion was low, and many people had been cooped up for a long time. A few residents' families were present, but mostly, it was just us elderly and staff. A firetruck was brought by the local fire department for the kids to climb on. There was also a bounce house and various games, hotdogs, and ice cream. I decided to add to the merriment or at least create a reason to be laughed at, something everyone needs from time to time. I found a clown costume and donned it for the event. As this was not a costume party, I stuck out like a rose bush in a field of grass.

I think I benefited more from all the smiles and chuckles than the people giving them. I ate snacks, conversed, and felt at ease, an almost foreign feeling by then. As the event lingered on, I felt my internal clock telling me it was time to get back to Gail. It had probably been nearly two hours, and she would likely be up from the nap I had put her down for when I'd left.

"I'm back," I said in a voice loud enough to be heard but not to wake and closed the door behind me.

In response, I heard a sharp gurgling sound coming from the bedroom.

"Gail?" I padded quickly through the entrance and living area. The gurgling had a different edge than the usual sounds she made. The closer I came, the more certain and terrified I was that I knew what it meant.

"Gail!" I entered the bedroom and found my wife, her face purple, hunched over and choking. I scrambled for the door, threw it open, and screamed for help. The CNA was there within a minute and performed the Heimlich maneuver while I melted into a puddle on the floor. The whole thing was one long, blurred moment. Gail was back, breathing, and rubbing her throat but otherwise unharmed. When I saw what she was choking on, I could have thrown myself off the roof. It was a piece of candy. My candy! Candy that Gail had never liked in our life together but that I'd still placed in my drawer to keep out of sight.

The CNA left me with instructions to give Gail plenty of water and to make sure I "Gail-proofed" the place again. I nodded silently while in my mind, I knew that was not enough. I had already done that. My wife wasn't going to die because I needed air.

I could never leave her alone again.

"My soul melts away for sorrow; strengthen me according to your word!" Psalm 119:28

Chapter Eighteen
The Eternal Flicker

I'm finding my emotional actions seem stronger at this time than say a few months ago. I just sit and look at Gail doing her thing. I say to myself, boy, I sure love that gal.

The last several months of 2019 were a steady stream of ups and downs for Gail. In the past, a peak or drop would be reached and last weeks or months, long enough to feel settled into a new normal. Now, the breaks in between grew less, and each drop deepened more than the previous.

By November, Gail's energy was anemic. I began to wonder whether it was weeks, not years, that I had left with my love. This was apparent to more than just myself as hospice care was returned to us, bringing the same competition of emotions that were present the first time hospice was suggested. But this time, I didn't fight it. I just continued rowing with the pulling of the tide.

Gail could no longer make it through breakfast without falling asleep in her chair, sometimes with a spoonful in her mouth. I would have to scoop the food out with my fingers to avoid another choking episode. There had been several of those over the previous months. The Heimlich wasn't needed again, but there was damage done to Gail's throat. This added to the constriction and weakening of the throat muscles, common among dementia sufferers, meaning that even a mashed pea could cause her to gag and sputter if not swallowed just right.

After her morning nap, on a good day, she might move herself slowly to her chair with my assistance. Other days, I had to move her by a sort of carrying-dragging combination. Once in her chair, she might stay awake for half an hour, at most, but more often than not it was only a few minutes before she was asleep again. At first, I tried to keep her awake. That was the standing advice from staff and various experts: dementia patients should be kept awake during daylight hours as much as possible to ensure better sleep at night, a closer adherence to the natural circadian rhythm our bodies need to function best—this helps memory retention, mood regulation, and physical restoration—critical in all persons but none more than people with cognitive and memory disorders.

In that first week of November, I was startled by new advice. With Gail's energy so low, it was now the better of two evils to let her sleep whenever and however long she needed. That change of strategy concerned me but not half as much as the next one— her sleep, even during the day, should be prioritized above eating.

"How will her body maintain itself?" I asked.

The pause and a face full of empathy on our doctor told me more about where Gail and I were in our boat than the actual answer.

"I'm sorry, Richard. It's just better that she be as comfortable as possible at this point."

I've never been one for denial. I've always felt and found that when faced with a problem, however great, the best course is to take it head on, own it, understand it, deal with it. The worst thing you could do is pretend it doesn't exist. I could never relate to people who attempted to pretend away their problems. The dragon will roast you whether you believe in it or not.

Until that point, I had never understood what it felt like to face a dragon so great, that I simply could not accept the reality of it. In the early days of Gail's diagnosis—when it was certain the path we would be on, that the woman I loved would slip deeper and deeper into dementia, fading away, piece by piece until she was gone—even then, I stepped directly into those dark, unknown waters, eyes open.

It was so plain on the faces of our advisers, people who had seen this more times than anyone should have to, yet the fact that my soulmate, my partner of sixty-three years, would soon depart this earth, depart my side…that was a monster too horrible to face.

Instead of accepting it, I resisted. Gail was not leaving yet. This was a hard stretch, but she was still here. Gail was eighty-two years old and suffering from Dementia, I accepted that. But I reasoned she would reach a new plateau, a new normal, and I needed to help her get there. We all need good sleep, adequate nutrition, and activity. I could make sure she got those things.

I redoubled my efforts to keep Gail awake while the sun was above the horizon, my sole occupation for the majority of every day. Then I focused renewed attention on her eating habits. I blended her food so it was as easy as possible on her metabolism and compromised esophagus. And I added flavor, lots of it—gravy, melted butter, salt, whipped cream—anything and everything to make each spoonful irresistible. Under my watchful eye, she drank the recommended amount of water and walked every day from room to room. This last part was agonizing for both of us because she was practically blind, and I was hardly able to support her. But we did it. That was what she needed.

No dragons. Only recovery.

This went on until I began to break down. I was so physically and emotionally exhausted that I began to sleep in late more often, something I had never done in my entire life. Still, I persevered—this was a phase. Gail would be back. On November 10th, she proved me right.

I woke that morning late and tottered on stiff legs down to breakfast while Gail slept. Lately, I had as much time as I needed. The goal was no longer getting back before she woke but getting her to wake when I returned. Upon returning, I found Gail already sitting at our dining table. I stopped in the doorway, determining whether this was, in fact, Gail and not a CNA come early to call. It had been months since Gail had so much as gotten out of bed by herself.

My Scrabble box lay open on the floor, its contents strewn about. Scanning the scene, I saw that the little black bag of letters was missing. I found them a moment later, or rather, they found me when Gail threw them, striking me in the chest. She laughed, "It's me and you!"

I hadn't heard such coherent words from her in the last many months. Her voice was that kind of playfulness, flirtatious in a way that seems almost mean-spirited if you were the observer, but the two engaged know it's for the other's attention.

"You and me," I said back.

Gail ate breakfast with no choking or wheezing. There was no nap after breakfast; instead, she wanted to move around. TTT was back, and I was in no capacity to keep up. I spent several minutes chasing her, always behind, until she fell and scraped her face.

"Ok, Gail. Less walking," I said. "Let's have some rest now." To which she smiled and spit toward me. I couldn't help but laugh at the absurdity. There was so much lightness in her, so much of the spunk I fell in love with.

Several times, I thought to pinch myself or dash cold water on my face, worried I was in some dream, or I had slipped into her world somehow. I decided against knowing. I would rather live there with her in this state we were both in than be in any other existence.

But it was real. When the CNA came, she found Gail as revived as I did. It was the talk of the place all that day, and several more staff members came to see the spectacle. They marveled at her sudden energy, saying things like, "That's one resilient lady," and "I've never seen anything like it." I was vindicated. I wasn't delusional. There was no dragon, no denial, just a woman who had needed care more than ever.

Gail didn't nap more than a few minutes the rest of that day. Or the next. Or any other for the rest of 2019. Gone were the days of long, comatose sleeps. It was as if God had reached His hand down and turned back the clock a year or more. There were still periods of choking and sputtering, but even that had lessened. We had done it. Gail was still fighting to be here, and I was there with her, giving her any advantage I could.

As 2019 came to a close, family visited for the Christmas holiday, and Gail was in rare good form, smiling and connected. I did everything I could to make our small place cozy and festive—splashes of red and green throughout the apartment, a small lighted tree in the corner of the living room, and Gail in her holiday best, even though her clothes hung on her fragile frame. Visitors came in waves, bringing gifts. When these were handed to Gail, her eyes would sparkle at the beautiful packaging, though she didn't seem to know quite what to do with it. Between gifts, she would sometimes stare off for a moment, but more often she engaged in small ways with the people in front of her with a clasped hand or a pat on the shoulder or cheek. She even was able to enjoy one of Stephen's famous Christmas cookies, something I monitored very closely. She coughed once, but there was no gagging.

If Gail was not in complete recognition of our guests, she was at the very least present with them. From where we had been just weeks before, I could not have imagined a better ending to such a difficult year or a more hopeful launch into the next one. Never had the glow of the holidays warmed me so fully.

Then, just like in the stories we read as children, the dragon awoke. It was the year 2020.

"And we know that for those who love God all things work together for good, for those who are called according to his purpose."
Romans 8:28

Chapter Nineteen

In Sickness and in Health

Fear, yes, I must admit I am feeling the fear of facing my life without Gail. I have never been one to look evil or sadness right in the eye. Avoidance has been my norm.

Everyone has their own memory of that year. They will all look back on it and say things like, "I was just graduating high school when everything changed," or "It was all such a blur, the virus came, and then a year had passed." Most of these memories will center around the onset of the new strain of Coronavirus, COVID-19, the factions that formed, and the information and misinformation presented by various leadership organizations, the predictions, the hardship, and death. Most will look back on 2020 and shake their head, shake their fist, or simply shake.

The year started for me like it did for most others, a continuation of the previous, a stacking of days that felt much like the ones that had come before them. Gail was still suffering from Dementia, I was still old and doing my best to take care of her needs, family still visited when they could, and my age was becoming more apparent each passing week.

A blow to my ego came when I was forced, after much stubborn resistance, to have several of my remaining teeth removed.

The pain had grown severe and nearly constant, the worst when eating. That was nothing new to me. Until I had a fever or couldn't focus, I would grin and bear these as nuisances, not emergencies. But the threat to my long-term health ultimately forced my hand, with Darlene insisting that if I waited much longer, infection could enter my bloodstream and then my heart. I would be gone, and Gail would be alone. I could not allow that.

For the next two weeks—down seven teeth and only three remaining from the previous extractions—I waited anxiously and self-consciously for my new dentures to arrive. I hated the thought that if Gail had a moment of clarity and gazed at her husband, she would see a sunken mouth gabbing back at her. I was tempted to slip into self-pity, but I would think about Gail and remember how insignificant the appearance of my mouth was compared to all other things we'd dealt with.

I took a steadying breath and tried to focus in a different direction, life before dementia, but for the first time, I could not. I strained to remember the feeling of waking to my equal partner, of what a long conversation with Gail felt like, of what I felt like as her man. Each thought eluded me, like my memories were hiding at the bottom of a deep, murky lake. I strained and reached out for them, seeing the faintest outline, but no more.

My heart raced, irrational fear suddenly gripping me. I got up and went to the bathroom, as much to hide my alarm from Gail as to see my own face and remind myself that I was still, indeed, me—Richard, a strong man, provider, rower of the boat. That's not who was staring back from the mirror. I saw a sunken face on a frail body. The fact that I was aging was not some new revelation, no. For the first time, I felt that I was nearing the steep edge of my own decline, that I might not live to keep the only promise that mattered, to be there with Gail until the end. That fear was only made more real in the coming weeks.

When the first news of the virus came to Victory Centre, the response was the same as it would have been for any flu-like ailment. Staff were monitoring the situation. It would likely be nothing of great concern, just a thing to be aware of and, if necessary, steps would be taken. I admit, I didn't pay any more attention than any previous flu season. I'd lived through eight decades of them, and we would do as we had always done. My body had given me reason to trust its resourcefulness against viruses. All my attention was split between caring for Gail, ensuring she had what she needed during this new viral season, and nursing my own "poor me" attitude back to health, tasks I struggled to accomplish well.

In late January, I received my new dentures and smiled a hollow smile back at myself in the bathroom mirror, a thing that mattered to only one person, certainly not to the only person that really mattered. And in the time it took for my false set of teeth to arrive, Gail had begun to decline again.

Pureed food held no interest to her, no matter how much doctoring I did to it. I had to force her to eat. Sleep had also infiltrated back into the daylight hours, more than in the waning months of the previous year, lasting between sixteen and twenty hours each day. And her weight, something she had already so little of to hold onto, started shedding at an alarming rate.

When awake, Gail was still active but moved around our apartment in a confused state. It was almost like watching the movements of a puppet being strung along by some outside force. I no longer felt Gail there with me. Later, I wondered if those last flickers of Gail were a final attempt to recover, a last grasp on the fading rope of her life before the light permanently turned off. I know now that this sudden increase in physical exertion is not uncommon for dementia sufferers toward the end. It is more closely related to the twitchy movements the body makes after the heart stops beating, more than any kind of conscious effort.

"For all intents and purposes, what's left of Gail has gone," said the doctors. "The disease is running its course. It's time to plan for the end."

I was handed a pamphlet, "Gone from My Sight: The Dying Experience," to help me understand what Gail's body would go through during her final days. It was just a few pages long, but I could never read through it. The dragon had returned, but once again, I wasn't ready to face it. I set the pamphlet aside with the intent to give it to Darlene during one of her visits. She was always better with those types of things.

One day during that Spring, I made a quick trip to the restroom and while washing my hands, I heard a boom and felt the vibration. I moved with an urgency fueled by adrenaline and found Gail once again on the floor in the closet, writhing in pain. The rest is a blur to me. Hospice workers and EMTs came. She was moved to the bed and checked for injuries and mobility impairments. Waiting for news felt like a long-held breath. When it finally came, the thing I'd feared for some time took the breath I held out of me. She had a broken hip.

We were already in isolation by then. The first wave of COVID was nearing full swing, and senior living facilities were the first to experience full-scale lockdowns. Due to the limitations of our situation, we had already been nearly apartment-bound before the virus. When hospice told us they could not recommend surgery for Gail's hip, I asked if things were really that bad out there.

"It is, it is…" said the hospice nurse. "But…that's not our chief concern. Mr. Sonnichsen, we worry that… We feel strongly that the chance of Gail surviving surgery is low. We think it's better, for her, if she remains at home…in as much comfort as possible."

March 24th came only a few days after Gail's fall, and I woke not knowing just how to feel. Sixty-four years, that's how long Gail and I had been married on March 24th of 2020. I wouldn't allow myself to think this might be the last time we celebrated our wedding or how it had really only been me celebrating it for the both of us these last few years. Rather, I spent some time just looking at Gail in her bed, trying to remember the different versions of her and me through the years. They came like half-remembered images from a movie more than pieces of my actual past, but I knew they were ours and smiled. I let Gail sleep as long as she wanted that morning. I had a quiet breakfast and received a call from a cousin I had performed the marriage ceremony for, just seven years after our own wedding. That was the first of many calls that day, more than any anniversary I could remember. Friends, family, past coworkers—it was an outpouring of love I wished Gail could have experienced.

Staff came with flowers and took pictures of us, Gail lying in bed with me standing beside it. When they were finished, Gail gave a weak smile and said, "That was nice." She was asleep before they even left. She slept through the rest of the day until it was time to take her meds.

For me, it was both the most meaningful and difficult anniversary of our marriage. I asked Darlene to make a poster for us, an enlarged picture of Gail and me with the words, "I Love You— Happy 64th Anniversary." I placed it in our window overlooking the Victory Centre entrance where everyone could see it. But Gail wouldn't know it existed. Her nerves were still firing, her lungs and heart still pumping, but my wife was not really there.

I craved her. I craved us. I wanted to pick her up and carry her around the apartment and listen to her laugh, then get serious and demand I put her down. I wanted to take her out for a beautiful dinner. I wanted to dance with her and then take her to bed. Everything I wanted was a stab to my heart. They were things I knew I would never have again. But there was one thing I kept, and we had it together. A vow.

I had promised Gail my life those sixty-four years ago, March 24th, in a little church. In front of our family and friends, I said those enduring words, "in sickness and in health." I made that promise in front of our God, and as long as our hearts continued to beat, as long as we continued to wake each morning, however briefly that remained for us, that vow was still just as real as the day I made it. As long as I continued to honor that, Gail was my wife, and I was her husband. I was hers, and she was mine. That would always be.

"But they who wait for the Lord shall renew their strength; they shall mount up with wings like eagles; they shall run and not be weary; they shall walk and not faint." Isaiah 40:31

Chapter Twenty

Waves upon Another Shore

She will always be the love of my life and I'll always miss her.
Life without her will never return to any kind of normal.

We were in the final hours. Victory Centre was in total lockdown like many of the senior living and assisted care facilities across the nation. Despite this, after much begging and promises of mask-wearing from myself and Darlene, we managed to gain permission for a limited number of family members to visit Gail. I can only imagine the pain and frustration Darlene must have felt, knowing her mother was fading away and not being allowed to see her or give her and me comfort.

Gail was heavily medicated, mostly dozing in her bed when visitors were permitted. She opened her eyes halfway when they arrived, but she was not there; these were only reflexes. I played Giovanni in the background, a mainstay for both of us during our time at Victory Centre, though I wonder now how much of it was for me and whether she heard the music at all.

Different reactions were plain on each family member's face, and I saw something of myself in each of them. Love, sadness, relief. I judged and understood each one as I judged and understood them in myself.

I also worried that the hospice workers, fully covered in personal protective equipment, would be a detraction from the family visit. They had been in and out of the apartment since Gail's fall, checking her pain levels, administering pills and patches, cleaning her, changing her, adjusting her position in the bed, all the things I had been doing for so long. But this didn't upset me; actually, the opposite was true. They had become family. It was plain that they cared for Gail and me. I supposed that was why they entered the field in the first place; they each had such a great capacity for empathy.

I thought about just how afraid I had been when hospice was first thrust upon Gail and me. I thought it would be the enemy of the boat, a great wave sent to spill us into the deep depths of the abyss. But hospice was more like a lighthouse, sent to guide our path through the treacherous shoals.

After the rest of our visitors left that evening, Gail labored through the night, her breath rattling coarse and wet. I slept in short, broken fits. Each time I'd wake with a startle and listen for the sounds that meant Gail was still with me.

When the light came in through the small window in our room, I sat up and checked again, and she was still breathing but not so loud. I kissed her, and her eyes barely fluttered. I said her name, and the steady breathing was her only answer.

Hospice workers came and went, but there was something different about how they moved from door to bed, bed to door. Their movements were guarded, rehearsed almost, like a ceremony was taking place. I looked the other way.

I managed to force a small lunch past my minimal appetite, then checked on Gail. Her breathing had quickened a little. The nurses told me it would get faster still. I moved my wooden glider rocker beside her bed and held her hand. It was delicate and frail with none of the strength it had always had, and I could feel the warmth slowly receding like a dying ember. There was no response to my touch, just breathing.

The day passed much the same until the pain of sitting too long and the pain of waiting made me get up and pace. That evening, I found myself flipping through channels, but I didn't really see the programs that were showing. I felt like I was slowly suffocating in the long quiet of waiting, waiting for something I didn't want to come, and yet there was always still a weight in the room, a presence of what was left of Gail. I feared the moment, having heard others relate their stories of losing loved ones. Not knowing what I would experience was more frightening. Would I feel her presence with me before she left? Would I only feel her absence? I felt like the Gail I knew was gone, but there was still the finality of it to come. I finally turned off the TV, and I've never heard such a deep silence in all of my life as the one that filled the apartment. I knew without getting up.

She was gone.

Tears filled my eyes before I stood, blurring my vision. I managed to take a breath through catches in my chest, then walked over to Gail. There was no sound of breathing. Her facial muscles were relaxed, more relaxed than I had seen since we were children. Her eyes were fully open, almost as if she'd been watching me and knew I would come and stand in exactly that place. The lines of worry and strain etched deep in her face from years of life were softened, and though her skin was absent of life, she appeared serene. Her burden was lifted from her. There would be no more suffering, no more sickness. Gail was in her eternal home without the cares of this world.

I leaned over her and kissed her head and whispered, "Farewell, my love. Until we meet again." Then I clasped my hands together and bowed my head. "Lord, thank you for the time you gave us. Thank you for this beautiful woman you gifted me. Keep her until I can be with her again. Amen." Then I wept quietly, for Gail and for me.

I touched her face, and it was pale, but there was still a trace of warmth. I waited some time before summoning the nurses. I needed that time, just me and her. After nearly eleven years of caring for Gail during her burden of Dementia, eleven years of witnessing the decline, somehow the final days still came upon me unprepared. I don't think there were any symptoms or behaviors, any rate of deterioration that Gail could have exhibited that would have made me feel the impending end. The monster we fear is often a patient one, making sure its shadow slowly blocks out the sun, not making itself suddenly known. No matter how large it became or how close it approached, I kept my eyes turned away. But it was always there, like anything we force ourselves to avoid. In that sense, I had always felt its presence while avoiding its terrible gaze. After eleven years of diligent care, a terrible void was left. It was truly frightening.

Yet within that agony, there was also a tangible peace, and I praised God for this. We had made it. I had gotten her safely to shore. I knew the angels were rejoicing in heaven with the arrival of such a beautiful soul. I only hoped God would soon greet me with a "well done, my son."

Gail's final act of love was to spare me the moment of watching her take her last breath. I think she knew it would have broken me. I took my wife's hand and knelt to lay my head on her chest for a few moments. There was no more pain, no more confusion and fear, no more struggle for my Gail. She was in perfect peace, the final new normal. We had stayed the currents, rode out the storms, and I had seen my lady to heaven's shore.

She was walking up that beach now. I closed my eyes, and I could see her, a bright light shining. She didn't turn back to me, but I knew she was smiling radiantly. She knew, and I knew. I would see her soon.

Gail Ferry Sonnichsen; Born June 14th, 1937; Departed March 31st, 2020.

Fly unhindered now, my dove. I'll find you in a little while.

"I have fought the good fight, I have finished the race, I have kept the faith." 2 Timothy 4:7

Wed, April 1   2020

This is the first day of a new journey, without God at my side it's a wonderful day. No more blank stares, no more hard breathing, pain when moved. This lady is right now at a place of peace and comfort at a place foreign to us. Oh the family and friends who have grown to love the magnificant loving, carring smile you just can't buy no matter the cost of such a beautiful partner I have shared 64 years plus

GOD BE PRAISED.

Epilogue
Boat in the Harbor

*Written by: Darlene Fuchs, Richard and Gail's
oldest child and only daughter.*

I vividly recall the circumstances surrounding my mother's funeral. It was a somber occasion, limited to immediate family members, a fact that evoked mixed emotions, both a blessing and a curse. Knowing there were countless individuals who deeply loved her brought me solace. They would have been present to mourn our loss had it not been for Covid-19 restrictions. It dawned on me that many of them had only interacted with my mother as her dementia progressed, never truly knowing her before that. Witnessing their expressions of condolence would have been emotionally challenging. Undoubtedly, this would have presented a significant burden for my father as well.

On the third of April 2020, as we arrived at the funeral home, a sight awaited us that evoked profound emotions. Amidst the biting cold, Vicky and some of the CNAs stood outside, their pink fingers firmly holding up a handcrafted sign that carried the heartfelt message, 'We love you." What struck me even more were the myriad of personal notes adorning every inch of the sign, a touching tribute from each staff member honoring the memory of my mother. The sight of their thoughtful gesture left me and my dad deeply moved, a testament to the profound impact my mother had made on those who cared for her.

Tears glistened in their eyes as they handed the sign to my father, their words of comfort mingling with the crisp morning air. Their genuine wish for the staff to be present at the funeral was evident. However, the harsh reality of the pandemic and its restrictive measures deprived them of the opportunity. Nonetheless, their virtual hugs carried a warmth that touched me deeply.

The atmosphere at my mother's funeral was solemn and serene, as is often the case on such occasions. The front of the small parlor was adorned with an array of floral arrangements, their blooms seemingly sprouting around the opening of her casket. Mom looked radiant, her hair styled elegantly, dressed in a simple white blouse and a purple cardigan that complemented the pastel flowers. A delicate pearl necklace adorned her, adding a touch of grace to her appearance. Seated beside her was her cherished doll, clad in matching purple attire, as if symbolically accompanying her on the upcoming journey.

Seven of us, along with the pastor from Village Church, formed a semicircle in front of the casket, creating an intimate gathering free from intrusions or condolences from outside parties. It was a space solely for us to share stories, memories, and words of encouragement. During the service, I seized the opportunity to express to my father how proud I was of him for the way he had cared for my mom. Witnessing his selfless act of love was truly incredible. He rarely showed frustration, except when his desire to do more for her collided with the limits of his abilities.

As the service drew to a close, I sensed a mix of uncertainty filling my dad's thoughts, "What now?" Yet, amidst the uncertainty, there was reassurance in the unwavering support we provided.

Following the funeral, my father decided to stay with us, sparing him the need to undergo the mandatory two-week isolation at Victory Centre. Given the circumstances he was grappling with, we believed that being surrounded by family during this time would be more beneficial for his well-being. We hoped that the shared moments and the solace of our presence would offer some measure of healing. Looking back, I realize that the experience might have brought more solace to me than to him, as he continued to carry the weight of his grief and inner struggles.

Throughout those weeks, my dad sought comfort outdoors, spending hours rocking in a patio chair under the warm sun, even when the wind carried a crisp chill. He established a daily routine of walking on the golf course, claiming it helped clear his mind. However, I sensed a deeper purpose behind those walks—a desperate attempt to ease the emotional aching. Unbeknownst to him, we could hear his anguished screams directed at God each day, even though he thought he was out of earshot. The raw pain in his voice was a stark reminder of the depths of his inner struggles and the profound burden he carried in silence.

Day after day, he set off from our home, adjacent to the twelfth tee, trekking a full mile to reach the southwestern edge of the course. There, at a break in the tree-lined boundary, he would stand for a few precious minutes, his gaze fixed on the building he knew so well, Victory Centre. Then, he would turn and retrace his steps.

Upon returning, I would gently ask if he had a good walk, and he would force a smile, offering some lighthearted comment about the weather or the picturesque scenery. He tried his best to shield me from the pain he carried within, determined to remain the father figure, strong and protective, for his child.

Witnessing my father's suffering was heart-wrenching, made even more difficult by his apparent emotional shutdown. Throughout my mother's dementia decline, he would confide in me about the tremendous honor and the challenges of caring for her. Now, despite our frequent conversations, we remained confined to surface-level topics, discussing the weather or mundane daily activities like meals. The deeper matters, the unspoken truths and shared vulnerabilities, remained untouched, as if tiptoeing around them would preserve the fragile balance we had established. The spark that once defined him, the one recognized by everyone who knew him, had seemingly faded away, leaving a void, an emptiness.

Four weeks after Mom's passing, as I was preparing breakfast in the kitchen, Dad walked in and stood there in silence. Concerned, I asked him, "Are you OK?" A brief period of silence ensued, my father choosing to withhold his words for a little longer. The weight of his emotions lingered in the air before he eventually broke the silence.

"It's just..." he paused, struggling to find the right words. "I need to go back to our apartment."

I couldn't help but notice the use of the word "our." It tugged at my heart.

"Of course, Dad. After breakfast, I'll drive you by there. Would that be alright?" I offered, hoping to ease any worries or reservations he might have.

He shook his head gently, his eyes filled with determination. "Not just by, sweetie. I... I need to go back. I need to live there."

His words hung in the air, heavy with the weight of his undeniable desire to return to the place they called home. In that moment, I understood the profound significance, and without uttering a single sound, I nodded in silent agreement, recognizing the vital role this decision would play in his journey of healing.

Pausing what I was doing, I attentively focused on my father as he shared his thoughts, revealing the deep emptiness and intense loneliness he felt. Despite reassuring words about his well-being, my father's yearning for the past was unmistakable. He desired to spend his remaining days embraced by the nostalgic memories he and my mother had woven together throughout their lives. There was a resolute tone in his voice that made it evident: this was not a matter open for discussion. I understood the unspoken truth, that with the raging pandemic and its uncertain duration, there was no guarantee that we would be permitted to visit him anytime soon.

We stayed in daily contact by phone, sometimes engaging in multiple conversations throughout the day. As part of our routine, the groceries he requested were dropped off at the Victory Centre entrance, where they would be properly disinfected and delivered to his apartment. Placing the bags down, a twinge of jealousy would wash over me, wishing I could personally hand them to him.

On occasion, we brought folding chairs and positioned ourselves in the grassy area beneath his window. From there, we'd look up to the second floor and see him peering down, his face filled with a mixture of longing and gratitude. Despite the physical distance between us, we engaged in heartfelt conversations that resonated through the open air. The absence of hugs and the inability to assess how he was doing evoked a deep ache—those precious moments were treasured.

We were delighted when the staff created a special setup for Richard and Karen. A table had been carefully placed, with enough space between the chairs, and atop it, the familiar Scrabble board awaited their game. Both masked, they could finally sit across from each other, ready to play their beloved game. Although infrequent, it provided a comforting reminder that they were not alone in their shared love for the game and, more importantly, in their fondness for each other.

I held onto the hope that my father's return would rekindle his spirit, but there was no such transformation. I believe his insistence on going back to the apartment was connected to a longing for closeness to Mom, a sentiment he had shared with me. Perhaps he sensed something deeper, something that eluded our understanding. Was it a final act of paternal love, shielding his children from the weight of his emotions? The questions echoed, leaving me yearning for understanding, seeking answers.

In mid-August, just over three months after Dad's return to Victory Centre, a phone call jolted me with the news that he was being transferred to the hospital. The tone of the staff person's voice left no room for doubt about the gravity of the situation. Test results revealed a blockage between his liver and small intestine. With no time to spare, he was prepared for surgery, leaving us anxiously waiting, unable to see him until the following day. The agonizing wait finally ended, but with a heavy blow: the surgeons couldn't remove the entire tumor. It had been growing aggressively within him for some time.

Contemplating this new diagnosis, I couldn't help but think about the immense pain he must have endured silently. How many times did he suppress a wince or cough into his sleeve, determined to hide any sign of his own suffering, all while selflessly attending to my mother's every need?

After an unsuccessful second surgery, I had to wait before I could visit my father due to COVID restrictions. When I finally got the chance to see him, he appeared groggy from the pain medication and visibly exhausted. Despite his condition, he mustered a smile when he saw me. Although I felt a surge of frustration, I restrained myself from expressing my anger at the fact that he had avoided addressing this condition, thereby allowing it to persist untreated for an extended period of time.

In a final attempt, the doctors opted for an alternative approach by inserting a drainage tube through the skin into the bile duct, allowing it to drain into an external collecting bag. Later, they discussed their plan to replace the external drain with an internal one. However, as I gazed at my father lying there with closed eyes, I made the decision to decline the surgery. Deep down, I knew he wouldn't survive it. It wasn't solely because his body may not have been strong enough, although that could have been a factor. It was his spirit that had faded away since my mother's passing, and his physical state was simply catching up to that loss.

The morning after being transferred back to Victory Centre from the hospital, I visited my father and found him peacefully asleep in bed. To my surprise, his drain tube was left partially uncovered by the sheet. Curiosity compelled me to pull back the sheet further, and what I discovered left me utterly shocked. The tube had become dislodged from his abdomen, barely holding on by a few stitches.

In that moment, my mind was flooded with a mix of emotions. Part of me was enraged at the negligence that had led to this situation, wanting to find someone to blame. But as I looked at my father, another part of me was filled with sadness and compassion.

His fingers, cold to the touch, gently wrapped around my wrist, and he mustered a weak smile. His gaze spoke volumes, saying more than words ever could. "No, my dear. No more. I've reached my limit."

When the CNA arrived to check his pain and wash him, I gave them the privacy they needed. As I retreated to the living room, the faint sound of a familiar melody reached my ears. It was the CNA softly singing "I Walk Thru the Garden Alone." And then, something magical happened. My father's voice blended seamlessly with hers, harmonizing with each note. It was the last time I had the privilege of hearing him sing.

Later, I reached out to my daughter Christina, and within the hour, she was by my side. With thirteen years of experience as a nurse-practitioner, Christina switched into clinical mode upon seeing Grandpa. In a loving tone, she whispered to me, "Now we wait. It won't be much longer."

Tenderly, she brushed her grandpa's hair, reassuring him with her voice that we were all coping and would find solace in time. Her gentle words carried the promise of a reunion with Grandma and Noah, urging her grandpa to embrace Noah tightly on her behalf. Respecting her private moments with him, I retreated, having already shared my heartfelt goodbyes. Later, in the hushed ambience of the living room, we spoke softly, sharing cherished memories as we navigated the bittersweet space between holding on and letting go.

In the early afternoon, Karen arrived, spending a few moments at Richard's bedside in her wheelchair. Grasping his hand, tears streamed down her cheeks, marking the first time in years that she allowed herself to openly weep, a testament to the deep bond they had forged over time.

As the afternoon sun cast a gentle glow through the window, Christina and I surrounded my father's bedside, holding his hands and praying. The room was filled with love and nostalgia as we played his favorite songs on his CD player. Time seemed to stand still. It was as if we had been granted rare moments outside the ordinary flow of time, fully aware of its fleeting presence.

Suddenly, my father stirred, as if a surge of life had rejuvenated his weary body. His eyes, bright blue and filled with a mixture of wonder and serenity, widened and focused on a point above the doorway. It was as if he had caught a glimpse of something beyond the veil of this world, something that brought him comfort and reassurance as he approached these final moments.

Christina, sensing the significance of the moment, turned on her phone's camera, capturing the scene that unfolded before us. It was a moment we could not fully comprehend, but we knew it was extraordinary.

With a grace that defied frailty, Richard raised his trembling right arm, seemingly reaching out to touch something ethereal. A radiant smile, pure and filled with joy, graced his face, transcending the confines of the room. The final word escaped his lips with profound clarity as he embraced the moment.

"Angel."

Richard Paul Sonnichsen; Born September 9th, 1936; Departed August 25th, 2020.

His smile brightened the world.

"His lord said to him, 'Well done, good and faithful servant; you have been faithful over a few things, I will make you ruler over many things. Enter into the joy of your lord.'" Matthew 25:23

Photos of Richard and Gail

Richard Sonnichsen
High School photo 1955
His classic allure is a
throwback to the
black-and-white era.

Gail Wagner
High School photo 1955
She embodies a timeless
beauty with a touch of
grace and charm.

Mr. and Mrs.
Richard Sonnichsen
Wedding Reception
Saturday, March 24,
1956
Clinton Baptist church
Two doves, naive and
innocent.

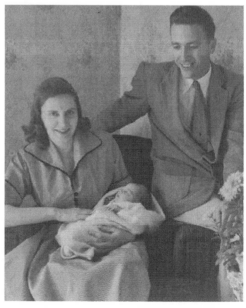

Embracing Life's
Journey: Darlene,
beloved first child of
Richard and Gail
Sonnischsen, enters
the world on January
8th, 1957.

Sonnichsen Family 1964
Richard, Gail, Carl, Darlene and Jeff
Answering the Call: A family of five headed
to Germany for their missionary work.

Sonnichsen Family 2014
Carl, Darlene, Jeff, Gail and Richard
Five Decades, Separate Roads: From distant
places and diverse lives, commitment reunited
them in the end.

50th Wedding Anniversary 2006
Golden Moments: Celebrating 50 years of
love, laughter, and endless togetherness
on their wedding anniversary.

60th Wedding
Anniversary 2016
Diamonds of Love:
Celebrating 60 years of
enduring togetherness
on their glorious
anniversary.

Richard (Papa) with Lauren,
Noah and Gail (Grandma) 2014
Generational Joy: The radiance of two grandchildren
illuminating the lives of their joyful grandparents.

Lauren, Gail (Grandma) and Noah 2015
Embracing Resilience and Love: In the lap of their
beloved playmate, Grandma, cancer warrior Noah,
alongside big sister Lauren, bring light to the moment.

Richard and Gail 2018
Moments of Connection: A heartwarming smile
of recognition as Richard holds Gail, the love of
his life on his lap.

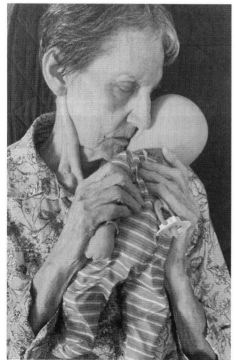

Gail and her "Baby"
2019 Tender Moments:
Gail cherishes her
baby doll, nestling it
against her face in a
heartwarming display
of love.

Well — HAPPY BIRTHDAY RICHARD
Mon SEP+ 9 2019
Let's see if my Birthday makes our activities even better — 83 years WOW
83 years old — 83 years married. At 85 a beautiful trip. Big smile from Gail. She? up and dressed, and ate a great breakfast. 'A Song of the day on Country music station ' 'She' a good-hearted woman — married to a good hearted man. What a birthday. No cake — No presents, but a loving wife who acted as she did as a teenager. I can't explain it, I'll attempt to write some. I'm writing this right after Gail and I returned from a 45 minute walk to the small park next door. All the way laughing, talking to me, wrapping her arms around me, even doing a little gig on the sidewalk as we went. Then sat on a bench in park, mostly cloudy, just a 10-15 minute peak of the sun which kept us comfortably warm. Sitting, her hands were all over, except one time she pulled my hands to her face and kissed them. At one moment 14 large birds flew side by side right over us. O he line-stretchy 30 to 40 feet left to right. Boy I said, I hope they don't poop on us all at once. Gail rocked back and laughed as loud as I've heard in a long, long time. We're back.

A page from Richard's journal. September 9, 2019
Richard's Birthday Reflection: No gifts, no cake—
just a loving wife's tender gestures fill the day.

Mon. Dec 2, 2019
Gail going early 6:30 – Loud and constant, I love it. I'm sitting at the table, immediately after I start writing she's up and over there at table, making herself known. She says out loud, "what I mean to say" (does she know what I'm doing") you tell me. After eating and clearing table, Country Music on, I do a little jig, she comes over to me, puts her arms around me and lays her head on my shoulder, and we do a slow dance. Then I go in to make her bed, and she comes in and actually tries to help arrange the blankets. What a beautiful start to the day. And she is still near me as I write this. Then Gail took a 45 minute snooze. And now I, t, t full speed as I sit here looking on for her safety. Today it has been more an observing day of Gail's activities. Very interesting. One was when she was sitting at table, I made a weird noise with my hand and mouth. She sat there, shielding her eyes with her hand, trying to figure out what I was doing. Then she comes over and kisses me on top of my head. I can't imagine what today's diary reads like. It's only up to 12:00 o'clock, and I'm dumfounded

A page from Richard's journal. December 2, 2019
A Remarkable Day: Filled with Gail's loving interactive
presence, TTT, and heartfelt affection. 'My old Gail was
back,' if only for a moment.

Acknowledgements

I would like to take a moment to express my deepest gratitude to the remarkable individuals who have been instrumental in the creation and completion of this book. Without their encouragement and enthusiasm, this endeavor would not have been possible.

To my beloved husband, Bill, you truly deserve a standing ovation for the undeviating support you've provided me throughout this incredible author journey. From patiently tolerating the countless hours I spent glued to the computer screen to actively helping me untangle the complexities of my storytelling, you've been my rock. Your steadfast belief in me has been a genuine testament to love, as writing a book can make one quite fixated! Thank you for being my pillar of strength and for always pushing me to reach new heights.

A special thanks to my incredible Street Team, Stephen Fuchs and Curt Grimes. Your constant interest and tireless support have been nothing short of extraordinary. From reviewing every step of this book's progress to creating an epic website, I am beyond grateful for all the effort you've poured into making this project a success.

In appreciation to my daughter, Christina, thank you for being by my side in the final moments. To my grandchildren, Lauren and Noah, who were always a source of radiant sunshine and pure joy, embracing their roles as Grandma's cherished playmates. And to the rest of my family: Sam, Jeff, and Carl. Your belief in my abilities has been a constant source of strength. Your words of reassurance and support have fueled my determination to overcome challenges and pursue my goals.

Kathy, my trusted confidant, your friendship and belief in me have been a constant source of inspiration. From the very beginning, you have been there, encouraging me to chase my dreams and reminding me of my true potential. Your presence in my life is a cherished gift, and I am immensely grateful for your steadfast support.

Now, to my dear friend Margita, for persistently inquiring about the book's readiness. And to the rest of you who have stood by me and cheered me on, thank you for being my sounding board. Your encouragement and camaraderie have lifted me up and kept me going. Your belief in my abilities has been an inspiration, spurring me to turn my dreams into reality. I cannot thank you all enough for the impact you've had on this amazing adventure.

For my wonderful friends who might have known about my book project and then lost track, I don't blame you; life gets busy. Now, as you settle in with a cozy blanket, prepare to embark on a journey filled with laughter, tears, and heartfelt moments within these pages. Here's to an unforgettable reading experience. Enjoy every bit of it!

With gratitude to my readers, your loyalty and enthusiasm have truly humbled me. The kind words and messages of appreciation you've shared have touched my heart and reignited my passion for storytelling. This book is dedicated to each one of you, and my heartfelt hope is that it takes you on an exhilarating rollercoaster of emotions, leaving you feeling uplifted and inspired. Thank you for being a part of this incredible adventure!

This book stands as a testament to the love, support, and familial bonds that have embraced me throughout this humbling journey. To my dearest husband, Bill, my ever-reliable Street Team, and all my cherished friends, family, and readers, I extend my heartfelt gratitude. Your unyielding belief in me has transformed my father's once-distant dream into a tangible reality, and for that, I am eternally and profoundly grateful. Thank you for being the driving force behind this incredible achievement.

I'd like to recognize the following individuals and groups who played a pivotal role in shaping this book. Thanks to:

Victory Centre of Bartlett, for providing a secure and comfortable haven for Richard and Gail. Your commitment to fostering a nurturing environment speaks volumes about your compassion and care for seniors.

Helen Brown, a steadfast confidant, pen pal to my father, and an invaluable source of guidance, played a pivotal role in ensuring Richard and Gail could live their best possible lives.

Karen, a cherished friend to Richard and an equally formidable opponent in Scrabble matches.

The dedicated CNAs and staff at Victory Centre mentioned in Richard's journals: Alex, Allesia, Amy, Brianna, Cara, Cynthia, Halley, Hanna, Hittie, Jackie, Joy, Stephanie, Kezia, Luz, Maria, Nancy, Naomi, Norma, Pam, Quebec, Ralph, Ruby, Sandy, Scott, Yessenia, Zee.

Comfort Hospice, the gentle guides aiding in the journey from earth to heaven.

Dina Haupt, my skilled massage therapist who skillfully relieves my fatigue and soreness.

Caregivers supporting loved ones through the challenges of dementia: Darcy and Greg Mowbray, Dagmar and Erich Freiberger, Elfriede Peters, John and Ruth Willis, Angie and Mike Kuilan.

The talented team of writers, designers, and editors, whose concerted efforts played a vital role in bringing this book to life.

And finally, I want to express my deepest gratitude to Shawn Dressler for forging a profound emotional connection to Richard's story. His collaboration and insightful contributions have unequivocally enriched the tapestry of this book. I am eternally indebted to Shawn for his invaluable insights that breathed life into every word of this narrative.

Moreover, I extend my heartfelt appreciation to Jessi, his wife, who stood steadfastly by his side throughout the evolution of "Get in the Boat." Together, they have honored Richard and Gail's legacy by encapsulating the bond that guided this narrative.

Made in the USA
Monee, IL
01 September 2023

18f9bdd9-559a-4f07-81d0-81dd2b530422R01